Farther Up the Lake

Note for Librarians: a catalog record for this book that includes Dewey Decimal Classification and U.S. Library of Congress numbers is available from the Library and Archives of Canada. The complete catalog record can be obtained from their online database at:
www.collectionscanada.ca/amicus/index-e.html

ISBN 978-0-9781357-4-4
Printed in Canada by Printorium Booksworks, Victoria BC

Powell River Books
Powell River BC, Canada
Book sales online at:
www.powellriverbooks.com
phone: 604-483-1704
email: prbooks@shaw.ca

10 9 8 7 6 5 4 3 2 1

Farther Up the Lake

Coastal British Columbia Stories

Wayne J. Lutz

2008
Powell River Books

To Bro...
My Friend and Mentor

The stories are true, and the characters are real.
Some details are adjusted to protect the guilty.
All of the mistakes rest solely with the author.

Other Books by Wayne J. Lutz

Up the Lake
Up the Main
Up the Winter Trail
Up the Strait
Up the Airway

Front Cover Photo:
  Powell Lake, looking north near Second Narrows
Back Cover Photos:
  Top – Float cabin, Hole in the Wall, Powell Lake
  Bottom – Powell Lake, south of Goat Island

Acknowledgements

Powell River Books, a small publishing company, relies on a few key individuals to support this author's writing projects. My steadfast editors are Sam Macintyre and Margy Lutz. Ed Maithus provides illustrations, and Bro teaches me how to relax. John Maithus, without even trying, contributes topics for stories that will occupy my chapters for decades.

Wayne J. Lutz
Powell River, British Columbia
May 1, 2008

Contents

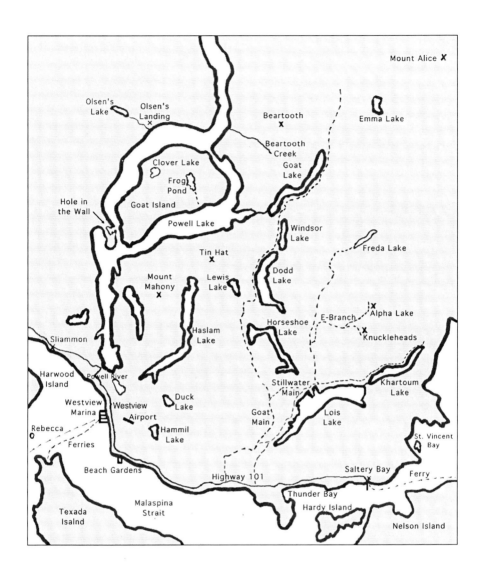

Mount Alice ✗

Olsen's Lake
Olsen's Landing ✗
Beartooth ✗
Emma Lake

Beartooth Creek

Clover Lake
Goat Lake

Frog Pond

Hole in the Wall
Goat Island

Powell Lake
Windsor Lake
Freda Lake

Tin Hat ✗

Mount Mahony ✗
Lewis Lake
Dodd Lake

E-Branch
Alpha Lake ✗

Horseshoe Lake
Knuckleheads ✗

Sliammon
Haslam Lake

Harwood Island
Powell River

Westview Marina
Westview Airport
Duck Lake
Stillwater Main
Khartoum Lake

Rebecca ○
Goat Main
Lois Lake
St. Vincent Bay

Ferries
Hammil Lake

Beach Gardens
Saltery Bay ✗
Ferry

Highway 101
Thunder Bay
Hardy Island

Texada Isalnd
Malaspina Strait
Nelson Island

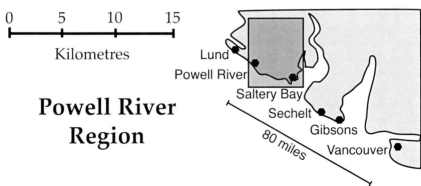

0   5   10   15
Kilometres

Powell River Region

Lund
Powell River
Saltery Bay
Sechelt
Gibsons
Vancouver
80 miles

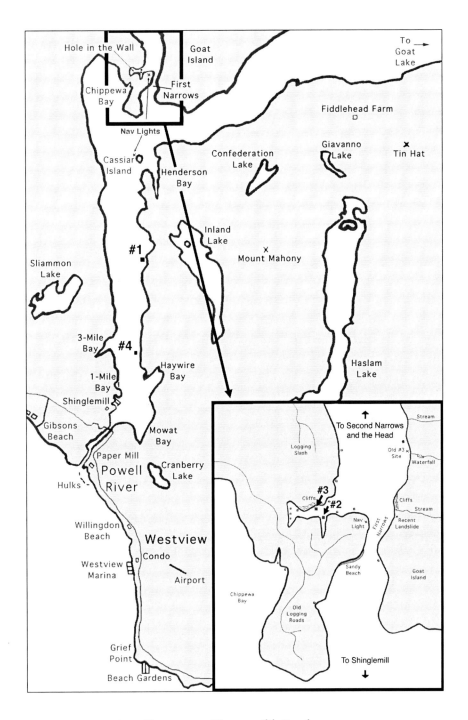

Lower Powell Lake

Preface

After *Up the Lake*

A s the sixth title in the series *Coastal BC Stories*, this book follows on the first and most successful of my books, *Up the Lake*. After writing the first book, stories of the lake kept popping up. I tried incorporating them into the titles that followed, slipping a chapter about float cabin life into a manuscript that was supposed to focus on winter hiking or boating on the Strait of Georgia. Not a single reader complained, but the stories that John continued to lead me into were too numerous to be relegated to a few chapters in a book about all-terrain vehicles or a work dedicated to aviation. So I began setting the new stories of the lake aside, awaiting the time when they accumulated to a critical mass. That time has come.

Farther Up the Lake evolved from a folder on my hard drive entitled "More Up the Lake," and that is really what it is. In this book, we'll travel to distant spots on Powell Lake, but the focus remains on Hole in the Wall, boats, John, Bro, and the aura of this wonderful place. In that sense, the stories take us farther in both distance and spirit.

The original *Up the Lake* generated a lot of interest among Canadians, but not necessarily within the small community of float cabin owners. The book seemed to appeal more to those who had never been aboard a float cabin. In the States, sales were meager, but an author can always depend on his friends to form part of the commercial audience. In Los Angeles, some copies of *Up the Lake* never left the coffee table of my fellow faculty members at Mount San Antonio College. But a few of my California friends actually read the book and attempted to understand my float cabin lifestyle. However, it's not so easy to identify with such a relaxed way of life when you commute daily for long hours on a bustling Los Angeles freeway.

Many of my city-folk friends who respected my change in lifestyle understood only so much. Many could not comprehend why I would move to a remote (to them) part of Canada and live in a floating cabin without a microwave or TV. When I returned to Los Angeles, one close friend would always inquire: "So how is everything with your house boat?" He knew I lived on a platform that floated on a lake, but that was as close as he could come to a real understanding.

On one return visit to California, I attended the wedding of a former student. It was a pleasure to see one of my fellow faculty members at the ceremony, and I knew she had actually read *Up the Lake*, and was struggling to understand the concept of life in the Powell River region. As a progressive woman in education and an accomplished pilot, she had come a long way in a professional career that is dominated by men.

"Are there many women up there?" she asked, as we sat together at the wedding reception.

"Oh, about 50 percent of the population," I replied sarcastically.

Which, of course, is true of almost any place on earth. But "extreme remoteness" was the mental image that *Up the Lake* brought to my colleague's perception of the region. Surely, most everyone is a logger, fisherman, or outdoor adventurer. And that implies few females.

Powell Lake is not as remote as a detached ice flow in the Arctic Ocean. As *Father Up the Lake* will attempt to explain, the lake is an exceptional environment, but it is also linked to a town and a robust community that is as modern as any.

Float cabin life occupies a special little niche in human history. Travel up the lake with me again. Let's go farther and look closer at this unique lifestyle. Yes, women live here too.

Chapter 1

Goat

Spring arrives with muted fanfare. The change of the seasons is a gradual process; yet the air has a distinctly different feel. Days grow gradually longer and perceptibly warmer, the sun riding higher in the southern sky. One day, the sun blazes between the clouds differently, boring into exposed skin with noticeable heat. The feel of the new season is in the air. Even with a brief regression to winter every few days, it is still evident – spring has arrived.

The new season is ushered in simultaneously with the spring hype in local garden stores that is associated with the end of March. The weather seems typical for this time of year, but plants and animals seem out of step for March, reflecting the residual harshness of one of the worst winters (2006-07) on this coast in several decades. Every aspect of nature seems to be delayed – the blossoming of flowers, buds on the trees, even the arrival of the swallows. By the end of March, I still haven't seen a single loon.

Last year, I celebrated the arrival of spring with a kayak trip to Harwood Island in near summer-like conditions (*Up the Winter Trail*, Chapter 18). This spring, I'm determined to enjoy a few overnight trips on the lake, taking advantage of the Bayliner, still in its winter float cabin berth at Hole in the Wall. The water of the lake has cleansed the hull and leg of this boat, which is normally moored in the ocean marina. Besides the advantage of the natural fresh-water rinse, the Bayliner provides an alternate source of transportation during the cold months. When the lake is rough, the 24-footer pounds through the waves more comfortably than the 18-foot Campion, my normal mode of transportation up and down the lake.

During the last week in March, a weather window opens briefly for a two-day trip on the lake. I've waited for a chance to anchor at the head of Goat Lake, and finally the conditions seem favourable. John plans to join Margy and me, although he'll be driving his own boat and not staying overnight. On any trip, having John along is like having a personal tour guide. No one knows these lakes and mountains better, and I'm always braver in my explorations when he is around.

Before John arrives at our float cabin, the weather forecast begins to go downhill. Without TV weather maps or the Internet to provide a picture of the major storm systems, I rely on a combination of marine reports over the weather radio and public reports from commercial radio stations. The ocean marine reports are worth my attention, although the winds reported on the chuck are usually more severe than those on Powell Lake, especially at Hole in the Wall. The mountains surrounding the lake break up the airflow, moderating the winds, except during major storms. Commercial radio weather reports seem reliable only when a major high-pressure system is parked directly overhead during the summer.

The 10:30 am marine forecast from the Pacific Weather Centre of Environment Canada has taken a nosedive since the previous report. Today should remain fairly calm, but winds are expected to increase tonight to gale force (34 to 47 knots), in advance of the next frontal system. Winds on the lake will not likely be that strong, but anchoring overnight in Goat Lake now seems an unwise decision.

But my heart is set on Goat, and I know John is already on his way up the lake. We're loaded for the overnight trip, so why not go anyway? We can explore Goat Lake today, and we'll be home before the winds usher in the next storm.

*　*　*　*　*

John arrives at Cabin Number 3 in his Hourston, swings his boat into the confined space of our breakwater, and pivots around in his patented 180-degree turn. As the Hourston drifts in close to the dock, John kicks the stern around in his normal display of precision docking. I have watched John dock boats for seven years, and I've witnessed only one minor miscalculation in his performance, when a swift current at Egmont required a second pass. Of course, I continually remind him of that momentary flaw.

"Change of plans," I yell to John, as his Hourston kisses the dock without even a thump.

I can see the disappointment in his face. John looks forward to trips like this one. He loves boats, he loves the sublime scenery, and he has anticipated the joys of a ride to Goat Lake as much as I have.

"What?" he asks, his voice showing a sense of concern.

"We're going to Goat," I reply.

"We were going to Goat," he says.

It's a little game we play, so now it's on again.

"But then we weren't," I say. "You haven't heard the latest marine forecast. Winds are expected to rise to gale force tonight."

"So are we going or not?"

"We're going. But Margy and I aren't staying overnight. So why don't we all go together in the Bayliner?"

John's eyes light up, a happy glow replacing the look of disappointment. He loves the Bayliner, as do I. It's not as fuel efficient as our smaller boats, but it makes sense for the four of us (don't forget John's dog, Bro!) to travel in one boat.

The Bayliner is ready to go, and so are we. Each of us occupies a customary place in this boat. We always defer to each other regarding our riding positions, as if they might someday change. They never do.

"Get her started," I say to John. "Margy and I will take care of the lines while you warm 'er up."

"Are you sure you want me to drive?" asks John, as if there is any other option.

There is no other choice. When we're in any vehicle with John, he drives. It's the way we all prefer. Not only is he the boat expert, his unique choice of navigational routes is what we look forward to on any trip.

"Of course," says Margy. "Let me know when she's warmed up enough to cast off."

John climbs up the ladder to the command bridge, pumps the throttle a few times, and starts the engine. Within a few minutes we're underway, as John maneuvers out past the Campion and Mr. Buoy Boy, the inflated racing buoy that has guarded our breakwater entrance for years. Margy leaves the aft deck, climbing up to take the seat next to John, but not before we go through more of our usual formalities.

"Are you sure you don't want the seat?" she asks.

"No, I'd rather ride on the stairs," I reply.

It's the truth: I enjoy riding in the standing position on the ladder to the command bridge, which brings me head-high with Margy and John. From there, I can duck down the steps into the cabin to check the fuel gauge, and then back out onto the aft deck to pet Bro. Only Bro, the fourth member of our team, doesn't get involved in this where-do-I-sit formality. He knows his place is on the aft deck, and already he's plopped down, head stretched over the side, watching the shoreline go by.

I stay on the aft deck with Bro until we exit Hole in the Wall. When I hear John adding throttle, I climb the steps to the command bridge and lean forward, bracing myself on the forward instrument panel to assist with the weight shift needed to efficiently bring the boat up to planing speed. I look down to the side of the Bayliner, watching the wake slip smoothly rearward to that magic point where it pauses, the bow drops smoothly, and we are on-plane. John adjusts the trim tabs towards the *Bow Up* position, the bow raises an almost imperceptible amount, and the boat settles into perfect cruise configuration.

As soon as we are established on-plane, Bro decides to go over to the other side of the deck, so John has to work frantically with the trim switches to keep our lateral balance.

"He always waits 'til I get things trimmed up perfectly," says John.

As if in defiance to his words, Bro walks back to the other side, and John goes through the trimming process all over again.

The view from the command bridge is tremendous, although we have to brave the cold spring air that flows past us. The sun blazes brightly, but the air is far from comfortable without protection. John wears a heavy jacket, his head covered by a faded orange-white-and-blue woolen toque, emblazoned with *Pepsi*. It seems like a strange way to advertise a cooling soft drink.

Margy is wrapped in a winter jacket worn over her life vest, a red *Canada* cap that makes everyone in town think she's a tourist, and a black set of earmuffs. I'm multi-layered, with thermal underwear, black snow pants with wide suspenders, blue baseball cap, red USC hoodie (forever a college sports fan), a winter jacket with raised hood, and my life vest over the top. I'm covered by four layers, including two hoods, and I'm still cold.

We enter the North Sea, so-named by John in recognition of the severity of waves on the wide-open water south of First Narrows. Today, as John points the bow at the new logging dock near Henderson Bay, the North Sea is glassy calm. It's a bit out of our way, but we can't pass a logging dock without checking things out, and today is no exception.

No boats are at the dock, and only one pickup truck is parked on the steep dirt road that leads up from the water. The boom area is empty of logs, and some of the boom sticks are missing, forming L-shapes rather than the typical rectangular log pens.

"Nobody's here today," I say.

It's a weekday, a logging day.

"They're done with this place," says John. "The guy who holds the lease for this spot is going to move his float cabin back in."

Such information is not unexpected from John. He knows things that seem unknowable. Where he gets his information is a mystery, but it's always accurate. Apparently, the cabin that was previously here will be returning after only a six-month period of logging activity.

"This was a big investment," I reply. "You mean they're completely done with logging here?"

"Oh, they'll be back. But not for a few years."

"A private company, isn't it?" asks Margy.

"Yes, they made a deal with the owner of the float cabin here," says John. "He moved out while they were logging, and now he'll move back in."

From Hole in the Wall, five kilometres away, I've listened to road building equipment and logging trucks throughout the winter. Sound carries amazingly well over water. Sometimes it seemed like the big equipment noises from this logging site were coming from John's Cabin Number 2, right across the bay from me. Now, after all that work (especially road building), the logging company has simply left.

We drift in the calm water a hundred metres from shore, looking up the steep logging road that drops directly to the lake. John maneuvers the Bayliner closer to the dock, then around an area of snags sticking up out of the water. At the top of one tall trunk sits an osprey nest that spreads out like a sombrero– nobody is home.

After passing through another small area of stumps, John brings the Bayliner back up on-plane, and we cross over to the Goat Island side for our cruise to Goat Lake. Goat Island, Goat Lake, Goat Main – particularly confusing if you use the shorthand I've become accustomed to calling them all simply "Goat." When I sit on the deck of my float cabin, I often refer to the wall of mountain (island) directly in front of me as "Goat." Or we'll ride our quads on "Goat" (Main). Today we're going to "Goat" (Lake), traveling along the shores of "Goat" (Island). It all makes perfect sense – to me, that is.

We follow the island's shoreline, weaving in and out at each indentation. As we approach float cabins, John steers farther from shore in respect for the log breakwaters, many of which have been severely damaged during the recent winter storms. Logs that formed parts of these booms now dangle to the side or have completely disappeared. We pass Bob's small cabin, recently refurbished, and Danny's larger seasonal home, still in the process of renovation. In both cases, these cabins have survived the winter winds without problems, protected in their coves, but others have been less fortunate. Some float cabins are noticeably tilted, their cedar foundations victims of the particularly severe winds that have ravaged the area. Our region is used to raging winter storms, but this year has been especially intense.

Major blow-downs are evident along the shore. Trees by the hundreds have been slammed to the ground, many projecting into the lake like toppled bowling pins. Looking up through slashes, more blow-downs can be seen at the edges of the open areas. One especially severe storm in December downed trees in a rapid-fire burst of energy. Goat Main was closed in several locations for weeks, an extremely rare event. The road to Khartoum Lake is still closed, the main bridge devastated by a raging flood of water.

We pass the logging dock at Narrows Main and the line of float cabins leading to Goat River (yes, another "Goat"). The water level is high now, but the stump-filled portion of the bay, near the river entrance, is still immense. What we see is not the problem – it's what we don't see, barely below the waterline, that can ruin our prop and destroy the leg of the stern-drive. John knows this field of stumps well, but still he motors slowly, keeping near the less-obstructed shore. A few red arrow markers help define the safe spots, but there are also lots of unmarked hazards.

Once in Goat River, the safe route is more clearly defined by the natural flow of the water. We wind along the tree-shrouded banks, the

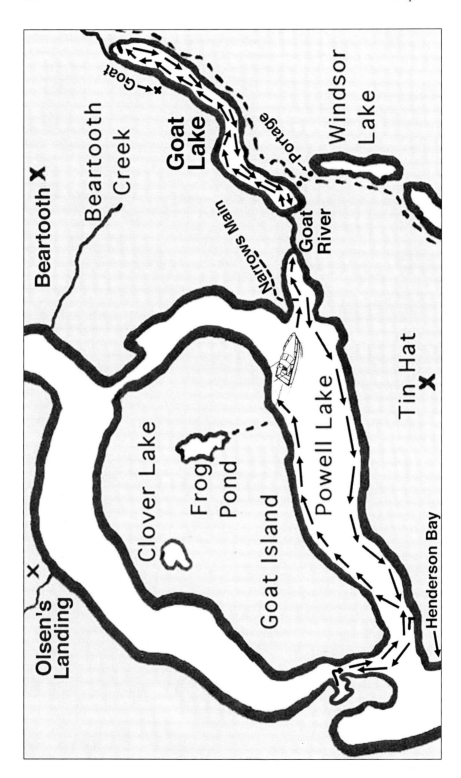

current barely perceptible as it flows out of Goat Lake into Powell Lake. The farther we go, the more likely it seems there is nothing ahead but a dead end. Yet I've been here before, and I know this narrowing river will eventually open out into Goat Lake.

Goat (the lake) breaks out between the trees in sudden splendor. The bright afternoon sun beams down on the wide basin – a lake within a deep canyon. Farther to the east, behind the first row of mountains, glaciated peaks strike skyward.

We pass the portage from Windsor Lake, part of the Powell River Canoe Route. I'd love to try paddling this course, but the portages would be impossible in our heavy sea kayak, so Margy and I would have to find a canoe for the trip. To view the entire chain of lakes (Lois, Horseshoe, Nanton, Ireland, Dodd, Windsor, Goat, Powell) by canoe or kayak would be a spectacular adventure. But the final paddle all the way down Powell Lake would be a killer. (I can hear us pleading: "John, please pick us up at Goat Lake.")

We cruise along the north shore of Goat Lake, looking up at a nearly vertical face of granite. Suddenly, John throttles back and points towards the top of the mountain wall.

"There's a goat. Do you see him?"

John's eyes are amazing. He can spot a mountain goat, barely visible against the cliff, while we're cruising at full speed.

"Help me find him," I say.

John is used to putting up with my less-discerning eyes.

"Do you see that dark patch of rock, just above that vertical canyon?" He waves his arm in the general direction. "Now go just above that patch, to the left a bit."

"I see it!" yells Margy. "The goat moved to the right."

"Sure did," says John. "He just jumped down quite a ways to the right. Do you see him, Wayne?"

I keep quiet. I'm searching frantically, and I'd like to see what John and Margy see before admitting defeat. But I don't see anything that's white and moving.

"Com'on. You've gotta see this guy. Oh, look, there he goes again."

"He hopped back up the cliff, to the left," says Margy.

I keep quiet, but I unzip the pocket of my life vest and pull out my small binoculars. With this magnification, I'm barely the equal of John's naked eyes. I focus the binoculars on the area to the left of the dark spot in the rocks. Nothing.

"Here, take a look," I say, handing the binoculars to Margy. "I'll get the bigger glasses."

Downstairs in the cabin, I grab the seven-power binoculars that should bail me out. Back on the command bridge, I focus them on the area where John and Margy continue to watch the mountain goat wander across the shear rock face.

"He's lying down now," says John.

That's with his naked eyes.

"I see him," says Margy. "He's huge, not at all like the skinny mountain goats I would expect to see."

With the small binoculars, Margy is barely John's equal. Now I'm scanning the suspected area with the more powerful binoculars. I nearly pass over a white blob that seems to be part of the rock, and then I realize it's the goat.

"There! I've got him."

Finally I see the mountain goat that John and Margy have been watching for the past five minutes. It's a lot larger than others I've seen in this area. He has plopped down on what looks like a sheer granite face, spread out comfortably in the sun, just resting. His shaggy, off-white (yellowish) winter coat has not yet been shed, making his bulk seem even bigger.

"He looks like a polar bear," I say. "Just lying there, waiting for something to happen. "

"He's huge," replies Margy. "Can you see his pointy, black horns?"

"Sure," I say.

She knows I'm lying.

After a few more minutes scanning the slopes, we don't find any other goats, so John shifts the Bayliner into gear and brings the boat back up to cruise. As we approach the head of the lake, a row of alders marks the entrance to the Eldred River to the left. A small wooden dock sits off to the right.

"Bob built that dock," says John. "He brings his boat in here and offloads his quad."

"A rather expensive way to go riding," says Margy.

Bob drives the biggest crew boat on Powell Lake, and his approach to quad riding is similarly grand in scale.

The dock floats a few metres from shore, lashed to a protruding stump. Apparently Bob backs his big boat in here, to offload his quad. Of course, Bob is a pro at driving a crew boat, and his twin engines tilt farther out of the water than ours. For today, we'll be content to use the offshore dock and our dinghy to get to the beach.

After securing the Bayliner, John rows our dinghy, *Mr. Bathtub*, to shore, with Bro along for the ride. Margy and I set up lawn chairs on the aft deck, and settle in. We munch on our lunch, sandwiches that are particularly tasty in this scenic spot, especially after a cold afternoon on the command bridge.

When John and Bro return, I have the three-horsepower Yamaha outboard motor ready to go. I hoist it into the dinghy and tighten it to the transom.

"Me first!" I say. "I won't be long,"

There isn't room or weight allowance for all of us to ride in the dinghy, so I'll go first. Once I've completed a quick circuit around the head of the lake, John and Bro will use Mr. Bathtub more extensively.

"Watch out – that thing is freaky," warns John.

Mr. Bathtub is one of our few pieces of marine gear that seems to concern him. I've been all over the straits and inlets of the region in this small dinghy – but very carefully. John repeatedly warns me about the limitations of this small, unstable tub. But his comments are coloured by the fact that he wants me to buy a larger and more capable Zodiac.

"Want to go?" I ask Margy.

"No, I'll stay here."

Margy isn't afraid of the dinghy, but she's content to relax in the sun on the aft deck of the Bayliner.

I speed around the head of the lake ("speed" is a relative term in *Mr. Bathtub*), exploring the shallow water area that is full of stumps. I shift my weight as far forward as possible, while still within reach of the motor's handle. I steer by shifting my weight, but the tiller is always accessible, just in case.

After ten minutes of exploring in the dinghy, I've seen enough to be satisfied, and I know John is anxious to investigate the outlet from the Eldred River. So I return to the Bayliner, taking a photo as I approach. As usual, John is chomping on a sandwich. It seems he's always eating when I try to photograph him: "Hey, John, hide that sandwich."

"I bet you wonder why I didn't go to full power," I say to John.

"Why didn't you?" he asks.

"That *was* full power."

Mr. Bathtub doesn't exactly push you back in your seat.

When I step out of the dinghy, John and Bro hop aboard, careful not to place all of their weight in the rear: "Now, Bro, you stay in front, or we'll swamp this thing."

Soon they're out of sight behind the alders, where the river entrance begins. *Mr. Bathtub* may be "freaky," but I notice that John is already maneuvering into a rushing river.

When John returns, we secure the Bayliner for departure. It's a quick process to remove the dinghy's small outboard motor and pull *Mr. Bathtub* up to its storage position on the stern.

Leaving the head of Goat Lake, we pass a big stump with an otter poised on top. Before we get close, it dives off its perch with a splash.

We travel on the opposite side of Goat Lake for a change of pace. Silver gray clouds are moving in from the west. The mottled gray sky, with the sun still streaming through in diffused strength, looks like approaching snow to me.

Farther west, back in Powell Lake, we pass a lone long-necked white trumpeter swan, swimming contentedly in the opposite direction. Osprey nest, mountain goat, otter, and swan – a rather complete day.

We stop to retrieve a blue 55-gallon barrel floating near shore. These barrels, used for cabin flotation, have popped free all over the lake this winter. They bob around, marking the aftermath of the fierce storms. The barrel we want to recover requires navigating close to shore. John slowly maneuvers against the cliff while I lie outstretched from the bow so I can grab the blue drum. Then I push the barrel back to Margy, who waits on the aft deck with a large fish net to grab it. John backs carefully away from the cliff, while Margy pulls the barrel along with us.

Together, the three of us hoist the barrel partly out of the water, using a rope around its circumference. By raising the open cap to the waterline, water gradually drains in giant hiccups (*glug, glug, glug*), until the drum is light enough to haul aboard.

When we finally return to Hole in the Wall, we make a stop at John's Cabin Number 2 so he can make a few adjustments to his breakwater. At the boom of old logs, John jumps out of the Bayliner and hops quickly from log to log (*plunk-plunk-plunk*) until he finds a log big enough to hold his full weight.

Meanwhile, I sit at the controls on the command bridge, maneuvering to pick him up. John changes the rope attachments on two logs and then hops again from log to log (*plunk-plunk*) and back into the boat.

"Home, James," he orders, as if I'm his limousine driver.

Of course, allowing me to drive my own boat with John still aboard is considered a privilege. I shift into gear and begin to navigate the short stretch across the bay to Cabin Number 3. I look at the cabin ahead and it's armada of boats – the Campion, John's Hourston, our tin boat, and *Gemini* (my floating writer's retreat). It's pretty crowded. To park, I'll need to pull in between the Hourston and the Campion.

"You drive," I say to John.

"No, it's okay," replies John. "You need the practice."

"Thanks, but I'd rather give it to you. Surely you don't think I can parallel park."

Neither of us thinks that, so John takes the helm again. It's a perfect parallel parking maneuver, as John slides in between the Hourston and the Campion. He uses a burst of reverse to kick the Bayliner's ass around, and we bump ever so gently against the dock.

Chapter 2

Storm Watch

Autumn on Powell Lake is a mix of ominous weather patterns, interspersed with sunny breaks. The leaves of big maples transition to bright orange and occasional red, their vivid colours weaving up the ravines of Goat Island. Waterfalls plummet down the steep slopes through dark swaths, sweeping their immediate paths clean of vegetation. In a few months, the downpours of winter rains will swell to become a melancholy stream of one storm after another. But, for now, the rain marks an exciting change of season.

Almost never does the precipitation of October extend longer than a week, leaving time for still-warm sunny days, with perfect temperatures for working outside. It's a time to cut firewood, prepare the floating garden for the winter, and enjoy the solitude.

At Hole in the Wall, Margy and I are the only off-season residents. Others come and go in the autumn, particularly on weekends, but seldom does anyone stay overnight. Yearlong residence at the Hole is limited to two Americans who came here nearly a decade ago and can't seem to ever get enough of float cabin life.

Nearly continuous occupancy in any season other than summer necessitates an ingrained appreciation of the power of the weather. For individuals who have lived most of their life in Los Angles, this is a place where the progression of the seasons can be appreciated.

Preparation for winter means learning from years past. The firewood supply is nearly ready for the cold months, although some additional cutting and splitting will be needed to top off the reserves. The wood cache inside the cabin is limited by its weight, a factor that must be considered in a home that floats on a lake. Too much wood inside, although convenient for rainy-day access, can submerge and waterlog our float foundation.

Other firewood stockpiles, subject to the same weight limitation, are stored on the porch. Kindling is stashed in an old Sailfish boat hull that is lashed to the deck. Bigger hunks are on the firewood float, tethered to the boat dock. Even more wood is stored in the shed and on the transition float, where it is rotated into the cabin as the need arises.

In the cold months, Margy and I move firewood in all directions, eventually reaching the inside storage bins for final drying, and then into the continually burning winter flames of the woodstove. As the firewood float empties, we cut more small logs from an endless supply that drifts in on the current, temporarily securing them to our cedar foundation with staples and ropes. Our home is a cabin that floats within the path of its own firewood supply.

* * * * *

Keeping the interior of the Bayliner dry is a lesson learned from last year. The boat is scheduled to move from the chuck to the cabin next week, where it will receive a reprieve after a summer of salt water. The

24-foot boat will augment the smaller Campion during the winter months, when the lake gets rough.

Last year, a particularly stormy winter (even by coastal BC standards) produced a constantly wet carpet in the Bayliner, the result of excess moisture everywhere within the boat. The problem became so acute that I began to think there was a hull leak, which resulted in a lot of lost time and effort searching for it. John helped me tear into the bow, disassemble the fresh water tank, seal the aft door, and inspect hidden spots throughout the boat. In the end, we never found a source for the water. Once warmer weather arrived, the Bayliner dried out quickly and spent the whole summer without further problems. This winter will be different.

What is needed, or so I am convinced, is a small source of heat within the boat. A 60-watt bulb should do the trick, as it does in our airplane during wet months. It's amazing how far a few watts of incandescent heat can penetrate. But to accomplish this, a source of electrical power is needed, not an easy task during the winter at Hole in the Wall. When we are present on the float, it is a simple process to manage our limited solar and wind power to keep the Bayliner supplied with electricity. But it is asking a lot to expect the same when we are absent, as happens during the wettest periods for as long as a month at a time.

The solution that I propose is an additional solar panel for the cabin to increase our winter power sources when the sun rides low. John designs a new selector switch for the cabin's solar panels that allows us to isolate the electrical supply to either the cabin or the Bayliner. When we're absent from the float, the panels will recharge an independent 600-watt battery power pack during the day, with sufficient electrical power to operate a 60-watt light bulb for a few hours each night.

While I'm in California, John installs the additional solar panel and a dockside box for the power pack. He designs an electrical switching system to isolate the power pack, adding it to the cabin's increasingly complex electrical system. My floating writer's retreat, a reconfigured boat named *Gemini*, has its own independent solar system, which can divert power to the cabin. A supplemental wind generator also contributes to the cabin's power grid. Now our winter power supply is enhanced even further by the new solar panel, including the means to keep a bulb going in the Bayliner.

When I arrive back at the cabin from the States, I test out the revised electrical system. All operates as expected, except that the battery pack is marginally recharged by the solar panels on cloudy days, and fails to operate the Bayliner's light bulb for even two hours a night. In fact, the power pack often drops below its voltage threshold, which sets off an alarm that consumes even more power. To make matters worse, the timer that controls the on-off cycle consumes more current than expected. All in all, the experiment is a failure. So it's back to the drawing board.

I abandon my goal of having a few hours of timed night heat. Instead, I opt for whatever power the solar panels will provide during the daytime, without a timer. If I can run a light bulb (preferably supplemented by a fan) during the day, all is not lost. Any heat is better than none, and a little heat goes a long ways in a confined space.

Between October storms, I run an extension cord from the dockside box to the front porch for my electrical tests. A small inverter provides AC that runs to a shop light and a low-energy fan that sit on the porch.

The light is draped from a rafter that allows me to watch it and the fan as I warm myself in front of the living room's woodstove. Under thinning clouds (but still no direct sunlight), the dockside connection registers half an ampere of current. The bulb glows, brightening as the sun breaks out from behind the clouds. As the amps begin to flow generously, the fan kicks on.

The brief parting of the clouds is followed almost immediately by a return to diffused sunshine. The fan shuts off and the light bulb dims, but the experiment is a success. Mr. Wizard, of old-time TV fame, would be proud of me.

With this new, small source of power to warm the Bayliner, the situation inside the boat should be vastly improved. When we're away, the cabin's solar panels will power the 60-watt bulb (sometimes even the fan), warming the interior and keeping it relatively dry. And the sense of satisfaction for doing it off-the-grid, in my own way, is an added bonus.

* * * * *

On a sunny afternoon in October, after a week of nearly constant rain, Margy tends to her garden, preparing the plants for the winter months that lie ahead. She trims back the asparagus and her wide variety of herbs, and prepares the strawberry beds by covering them with moss to ward off the impending cold.

A mysterious critter has been harvesting plants in the garden lately. Although we usually use our John-built pulley system to return the garden to its breakwater location during the evening, problems begin when we miss a night and leave the garden tied to the transition float. The next day, something has eaten off the tops of many of the plants, leaving them in neat piles.

Margy cleans up the cuttings and sends her garden out to the breakwater. The next morning, when she pulls it back in, the critter has struck again. A well-organized mound of severed plants sit on a garden stump, and past-ripe strawberries are aligned in a tidy pile. The mysterious critter now seems to be living aboard the garden.

I set a trap for the garden's resident, using a catch-and-release contraption with peanut butter for bait. The next morning, the trap

has been sprung, and a bushy-tailed woodrat (also known as a packrat) is inside.

The woodrat, a cute little critter with big ears and a squirrel tail, takes a ride with me in the tin boat. I choose a headland of rocks on the edge of the Hole's entrance, slide the woodrat out of the cage, and watch him cavort along the shoreline. He'll have plenty of time to regain his packrat hoard of winter greenery before winter sets in, but hopefully far enough away from us that he doesn't find his way back.

* * * * *

I use the few hours between storms to split kindling and bail out the tin boat (a never-ending process at this time of year). Then I climb the stairs to shore. Past the outhouse and compost pile, I turn left on the path to the neighboring cabin. I maintain this trail to park-like perfection, although I seldom hike it. In case of emergency, it's the only easily navigated land route from our cabin.

Today, all that is required is a light pruning of the trail, trimming salal, blackberry runners, and an occasional overhanging branch. When I finish clearing the path, sprinkles are already beginning to fall,

marking the beginning of the next storm. I walk back along the trail, returning to the top of the three sets of steps that lead down to the cabin. Water still tumbles down the ravine from the previous storm in a continuous flow under the stairs.

Autumn is a time of fast-paced storms, but today is a brief respite. In the cabin below, a warm fire and an early dinner await me.

* * * * *

When a storm moves in, the greatest danger is the threat of strong winds, although Hole in Wall is better protected than most places on the lake. Even when the Hole's winds are vicious, the float rides out storms well. The biggest self-imposed hazard is traveling on the lake in such conditions. When in doubt, wait it out.

During November, at our condo in town, I watch the latest weather satellite loop on TV. Storm after storm is lined up, well out into the Pacific. The surface analysis map is a mix of weather systems converging on British Columbia. An Aleutian low hovers over the Gulf of Alaska, not yet moving south as it would do in winter. Pineapple Express moisture streams in from Hawaii, and a small storm is headed directly towards the Oregon coast. The TV weatherman points to a low pressure center that is second in line, referring to it merely as "Ling-Ling." It's a small depression that displays closely wrapped isobars on the weather chart, a harbinger of strong winds. I conclude that Ling-Ling is an expended typhoon that's running on a rebound course from Japan. Almost anything can happen in the north Pacific this time of year.

The seas to the south are still warm, packing huge amounts of moisture. Warm air can hold more water vapor than cold air, and occasionally the stage is set for collision with an Aleutian low moving down the coast. Colliding air masses this time of year make the Raincoast even wetter and notoriously windy.

On Powell Lake, we ride out the storms. John has built a wonderfully strong cabin. Double cables anchor us to the cliff, and a strong cedar float forms a skookum foundation for an all-season home.

Most locals use their cabins only in the summer, so we are an exception. Staying overnight on the lake, as Margy and I do almost continuously, is extremely rare in the off-season (any season but summer). Most locals have no interest in increasing their exposure to the rain, but I relish it. As far as I know, there is only one other cabin occupied full-time during the winter (by the legendary Fritz and his dog, Shorty). Locals prefer to spend winters in their cozy homes in town. Some visit their cabins on a sunny winter day for a quick outing. Often, they are merely checking how well their float has survived the recent storm.

Thus, Powell Lake is a wonderfully isolated place in the off-season. On many days, the only passing vessels are crew boats or tugs towing barges or booms of logs. I watch work boats go up the lake in the winter's early morning darkness, and home again in the late afternoon or even at night. Unlike recreational boats, these hefty radar-equipped vessels are capable of navigating through darkness and storm. I hear their big engines approaching; then I see their running lights gliding past. My view, even in the dark, is like a continuous wide-screen, high-definition TV, with unlimited program content. The landscape remains fixed, but the weather and boats create an ever-changing visual show.

Hole in the Wall is normally one of the most tranquil spots on the lake, but it is not entirely exempt from the effects of autumn storms moving down the coast. November on the float is an awe-inspiring cycle of storm after storm. It is a safe place to be, if you treat the weather with respect. You need to keep an ear tuned to the weather radio, primarily to make sure you don't travel up or down the lake during conditions too windy for your boat and your level of experience. It's not the rain, but the wind, that demands the most respect.

On TV today, the weatherman turns to the long range forecast. Each day of the week is portrayed by a little cloud icon with rain falling. There is no end in sight.

* * * * *

In town, we sit and wait. Late in the day, the winds ease and the rain stops, but there is too little daylight left to travel up the lake. To-morrow morning, we should be able to make our break for the float cabin.

I set an alarm to get us going at a reasonable hour. But when I awake at 7 am, the dark clouds have already rolled back in. Margy and I get moving as quickly possible, spending little time at the grocery store, grabbing only those items essential to add to our cabin's already well-stocked propane refrigerator. If we are to utilize this weather window to travel up the lake, speed is essential.

By the time we load our boat at the Shinglemill, the southern sky is growing increasingly black, and it's beginning to rain. Breaks between storms this time of year can often be measured in hours rather than days.

We plan to make a necessary stop at John's Cabin Number 1. An old boat, open except for a tarp, floats there, and it is filling with water. I've promised John that I will bail it out on this trip up the lake. Without action soon, the next few downpours could sink the decrepit hulk.

We carry only one load of supplies to our boat, leaving some of the nonessentials in the truck for another day. There will be better weather ahead for transporting the extra provisions.

The trip to John's Cabin Number 1 is made through relatively calm water, although it now looks ominously dark in all directions. I maneuver the Campion into John's breakwater, rafting up next to the old boat.

"Why don't you stay aboard," I suggest to Margy. "It'll be pretty cramped inside, and there's probably only one bailing bucket."

"Okay," replies Margy, with a notable sense of relief.

She usually feels uncomfortable climbing in and out of boats in situations like these. I've yet to find a challenge she can't handle, but her footing is not always stable, so she's better off waiting while I attend to the task of bailing.

I tie our Campion to the old boat's swim-grid, which is partly separated from the stern and hanging precariously. Conditions here, behind John's breakwater, are nearly calm. This will take only a few minutes.

When I pull back the blue tarp covering the otherwise open boat, it's obvious that the water has not yet reached dangerous levels. There's lots of water in the boat, but it's far from sinking. I crawl over the side and walk the rickety aft deck to the gaping opening that marks the bow. Water here is about two feet deep.

This boat is a project looking for a purpose, and it hasn't yet become a priority for John. If he ever plans to use it for hauling quads, he'll need to reseal the hull. Although most of the water inside has entered through gaps in the tarp, some of it is has seeped in through the bottom.

A bailing bucket sits near the opening in the bow, with a rope tied to its handle, securing it to a cleat. I untie the rope and begin to bail.

Nothing gets old faster than bailing out a boat, especially when the water is deep. The bottom of the hull seems cavernous, and the gunnels are high, so it takes a lot of effort just to lift a full bucket over the side. I work by moving manageable quantities, filling the bucket half full, tossing out about a gallon at a time. I try to keep the bucket doses equal, so that I can estimate how much water I bail. Besides, it gives me something to do, counting gallons as I go. By the time I reach gallon number fifty, my arms are beginning to tire, so I take a brief break.

"You okay back there?" I yell to Margy.

"Doin' fine," she replies. "Just resting in a nice dry boat. How about you?"

"Okay. But not so dry here."

The tarp must remain pulled back to accommodate my body in the front of the boat, and now it's raining pretty hard. I'm dressed in a warm jacket, but it's not waterproof, and I'm sweating up a storm.

I return to the task, determined to bail a full hundred gallons, a nice round number. That will certainly be enough for now, since there is no danger of the boat sinking.

I only make it to eighty before I run out of energy. Taking another break would mean staying hunched over in the rain, so I quit. I retie the bucket and crawl out of the old boat, back into the Campion. I adjust the plastic tarp and cast off as quickly as possible. Margy assists in gttting us underway by securing the back canvas of the Campion while I motor out of the breakwater. It's tough to stay dry on Powell Lake during November.

* * * * *

By the time we unload the Campion at Hole in the Wall, the wind is beginning to increase. When you feel wind gusts in the Hole, it normally means a big blow is on its way. The bay is so well protected that it takes a major storm to produce winds above 10 knots. But the velocity can go a lot higher when a big cold front rolls up against the BC coast.

Late in the afternoon, I sit on the couch in the cabin, looking out through the wide glass door. The audiovisual treat through the glass today comes from the gentle movement of the cabin and the majestic view that pans across three waterfalls as the float moves outward from shore and then back towards the cliff. The orange-leaved maples at the base of Goat Island add a regal mix of colour to the magnificent panorama.

During the evening, sustained drizzle and a few brief gusts tug on the cabin. We ride outward to the full extent of the shoreline cables, bringing the cabin to a rather abrupt halt – a jarring *thump* that doesn't rattle the dishes, but reminds you that you live on a floating foundation.

As soon as we come to a stop, the cabin starts back towards shore. The ride in that direction ends when the float whacks against the stiff leg, a log that keeps the cabin away from the cliff – another mild *thump*. Back and forth we go, slowly and almost melodically, while the wind generator adds a background *whoosh* that builds suddenly as the blades spin up, momentarily adding a few amperes to the electrical system.

I watch the small Canadian and BC flags on the clothesline, as they drop back down, indicating that the wind velocity has decreased below seven knots. One final light *thump*, another brief *whoosh*, and the cabin comes to a smooth stop.

But the barometer is below 1000 millibars, and the trend is increasingly downward. The storm is still moving in, so this is only a temporary lull.

When I climb the stairs to the loft at 10 pm, the *whoosh* of the wind generator has returned, and the wind is distinctly from the southeast. I lay in bed, enjoying the familiar movement of the cabin and the sound of the wind, knowing I'm on a strong float foundation in a sheltered location. Tonight, the rest of the lake is undoubtedly a vortex of wind-battered waves on the open water. But here at Hole in the Wall, the cozy feeling contradicts the fury of this storm as it slams into the British Columbia coast.

The rain arrives in a blast of energy that pounds against the metal roof, only a few metres above my head. Big drops of rain ping loudly for several minutes, then diminish to a steady, soothing rhythm.

I fall asleep to the sound of raindrops tapping gently on the roof and the sway of the cabin as it rides back and forth, gliding magically through the storm.

* * * * *

At 2 am, I'm awakened by the sound of the wind trying to rip the metal roof off the cabin. Air is rebounding off the nearby cliffs in every conceivable direction, and rain blasts the cabin from one side, then the other. The wood frame of the cabin walls and floor creak in the strong gusts of wind, alternating with the grinding metallic sounds of the roof panels. I go downstairs to check my weather instruments.

The barometric pressure is still dropping, now at 990 millibars, and the anemometer's memory mode shows sustained gusts of 27 knots (50 kilometres per hour) within the past hour. That means the winds elsewhere on the lake are probably 80 kilometres per hour in the worst spots. This is no minor storm.

I stay awake long enough to see the barometer drop two more digital notches to 988, but the gusts are dissipating, at least for now. I fall back to sleep without further concern, although the front has still not passed.

At 8 am, I'm awakened by the wind again. But I can see a touch of brightness in the sky that indicates passage of the cold front. Although the barometer is still dropping, rapid improvement should follow. A reading of 980 millibars indicates the severity of this storm, and the shift of winds following a front can be rough for a few hours.

Sitting on the couch, looking out of the glass door towards the entrance to the Hole, I watch a small waterspout move north through First Narrows. Then another white tornado-like swirl, bigger this time, emerges from the Narrows, tracking north. The second waterspout turns abruptly to the left and heads directly into the Hole, and straight toward our cabin!

"Look at this!" I yell to Margy, who is just coming downstairs from the loft. "Two waterspouts, and one is headed right for us!"

In the disruption of the water near the entrance to the Hole, whitecaps splash every-which-way. Within seconds, the sun comes out and the wind drops away to nothing, a false sense of security. Yet the waterspout is still headed our way. Suddenly, the wind surges and the cabin rushes outward from the shore.

"There go the boats!" yells Margy.

In the confusion of the moment, the waterspout seems to have hit us. Simultaneously, both of our boats have broken loose from the dock, where they share a common dock ring. Each boat is now tied to the cabin by only a single rope. I'll need to act fast, but the deck is engulfed in a torrent of wind.

"The sawhorse is gone!" shouts Margy.

"Gone?"

"It just flew off the deck on the back side. There it goes, right out the entrance."

I look towards the breakwater. Both boats have swung out towards the boom at awkward angles. The large sawhorse, so heavy that it is difficult for me to lift, is now bobbing up and down in the water, and drifting rapidly out into the channel.

I slip on my shoes, quickly check the anemometer (a gusty 36 knots), and carefully slide the glass door open. When I step out of the cabin, the wind wants to grab my body and throw me off the deck, right toward the boats. I plant my feet as flat and as firm as possible, making baby steps towards the dock.

I'm able to grab the Campion's stern line, with the severed dock ring still dangling from it. I'm immediately in a tug-of-war with the boat, and at first it seems that the boat will win. But then I manage to pull the Campion closer to the dock, and secure the rope to a wooden beam under the deck. Then I do the same for the bow of the Bayliner, pulling with all my strength to bring the boat back to the dock. I win again, and manage to tie a quick knot to the same beam.

Now, with the winds noticeably decreased, I have some time to gather more ropes from the cabin and begin securing both boats in a more organized fashion. In a few minutes, I've tied additional ropes to other beams underneath the deck. It is a mixed assortment of lines, but it assures that the boats will stay in place for now.

Back in the cabin, I use binoculars to inspect John's Number 2 cabin on the opposite shore. The top section of his chimney is dangling precariously from the roof, but all else seems normal from this distance. When it's safe, I'll launch the tin boat to make a closer inspection of his cabin and scout the shore for the missing sawhorse.

Everything calms down quickly. The sun is out, and billowing cumulus clouds mark the passage of the cold front. The wind blows strong from the northwest for several more hours, but then steadily decreases in velocity.

The barometer bottoms out and begins to rise rapidly. By early afternoon, Hole in the Wall is nearly placid. At Powell River Airport, the wind velocity drops off from this morning's record – 124 klicks, a notch higher than hurricane velocity (116 kilometres/hour).

Cabin Number 3's dock is a tangle of lines running out to the boats. At John's cabin across the bay, the bridge from shore has been tossed from its tracks and hangs just above the waterline. John's chimney is in two sections, stradling the peak of the roof.

The sawhorse is never seen again.

Chapter 3

Fog Depositing Ice

I pace the docks at the Shinglemill, waiting for something to happen. I'm not your typical patient soul, but I've been trying to control my get-going nature for a full hour. My boat is loaded and ready to go, including two 20-gallon propane tanks, three bags of cabin supplies, a laptop computer, freshly laundered clothes, three jugs of water, and my backpack. I'm ready to go, but I'm still here.

Fog is not to be messed with, and it gets my attention. This is the fourth straight day of dawn-to-dusk fog. I'm anxious to return up the lake, and I'm exercising as much restraint as can be expected in this situation. Surely a boat will pull into the marina soon, the captain able to tell me what to expect regarding the conditions farther north. The fact that no vessel, not even a logging crew boat, has appeared in the past hour may be indirectly telling me something.

* * * * *

The fog moved in right after the last January rainstorm moved out. The long-range forecast shows sunshine for a full week, almost unheard of this time of year. But the high pressure area that has brought fair weather to the rest of the Sunshine Coast has brought unending fog to us. The TV weatherman says tomorrow will be another day of sunshine. He's talking about the rest of the southcoast, not here.

On each of the past three days, I drove Margy to the airport, awaiting the one o'clock Pacific Coastal flight to whisk her away to Vancouver. Three times we sat in the lobby together, waiting for the sound of an arriving airliner. The airport sits four hundred feet above the chuck, near the upper limit of the fog. Once in awhile, the sun shines through the fog for a few brief minutes. Then it is gone. In three days, Pacific Coastal has not landed a single airplane in Powell

River, but they keep trying. Meanwhile, Margy's trip to Vancouver is still on hold. Her next visit to the airport will be made alone. I'll be up the lake – I hope.

* * * * *

The fog at the Shinglemill comes and goes. More correctly, it almost goes. The sun breaks through, and the faint outline of land across the channel to the east and north improves for a few minutes. Overhead, the sky is actually blue at times. Then it is gray again.

Joe arrives in his truck to check on his houseboat. It's an appreciated diversion from my increasing impatience. We discuss the fog, knowing nothing about what lies to the north.

"I'm feeling better about navigating the lake these days," I brag. "Following the shoreline doesn't bother me, because I know Powell Lake a lot better now. But I'm always worried about another boat running into me in the fog."

"Most of the crew boats out there have radar," he says.

"Sure, but I doubt they'd see my fiberglass 17-footer. And what about other guys like me sneaking along the shore without radar?"

"They won't be going very fast," offers Joe.

True, but it doesn't take much speed for a big collision, especially if you don't see a converging boat until it is on top of you. Coming down the lake last week, I left Hole in the Wall in the clear, with sunny skies to Cassiar Island. That's where I hit a solid wall of fog and slipped into Henderson Bay to await improvement to the south. I shut off the engine and drifted for a half-hour, lounging in the sunny stern, watching the rapid clearing to the south.

Once underway again, I drove under clear skies all the way to John's Number 1 cabin. The wall of fog was once again in front of me, but the conditions across the channel looked better, so I slipped across and down the shoreline to Three-Mile Bay. At that point the wall became solid again.

After another wait, the fog didn't cooperate. This close to the Shinglemill on the western edge of the lake, navigating back into the marina seemed a simple process. Just follow the shoreline to One-Mile Bay and then into the docks.

I crept at near-idle speed, only 10 metres offshore. With One-Mile Bay around the next promontory, I loosened up a bit. Suddenly, a

canvas-covered boat jogged around me, overtaking from behind and swerving outward from shore. Did he see me at the last minute?

This boat was bigger than mine, but not a crew boat. His diverging path as he passed my boat indicated that he came up directly behind, maybe saw me at the last minute, and then broke off to the side. The boat then rapidly decelerated, as if in fright. I know it frightened me.

After that thought-provoking incident, I pulled out behind the boat and followed him to the marina. It was an easy trip the rest of the way, but it could have ended differently, a sobering thought that still lingers.

Now I stand on the dock alone, awaiting a boat from up the lake to report on the conditions. The sky is brightening to the north, but the nearby shore is still enshrouded in water-hugging clouds of fog. The sun forms a dim orb overhead, now dropping towards the western horizon. The air will cool further as the sun sets, leading to even thicker fog. I certainly don't want to press against darkness in a foggy journey like the one documented in *Up the Main* (Chapter 9). But I could take a careful look by sampling the west shore before it gets any later.

I launch, being careful to promise myself that I will go only so far unless the fog clears. The sky may open to sunshine only a kilometre north or it may be this way all the way to Hole in the Wall. I'll hug the western shore, go as slow as prudence requires, and make sure I turn back no later than Three-Mile Bay if the fog doesn't lift. I have the map of the lower lake loaded into my GPS, and I've unzipped the overhead canvas flap so I can drive while standing. My head pokes out of the top of the boat, allowing me to keep the shore continually in sight and to maintain a close lookout for other boats. It's a safe scenario, as long as I don't overstep my self-imposed bounds.

As I drive slowly northward, visibility doesn't improve. In fact, at One-Mile Bay, conditions get noticeably worse. I lose sight of the shoreline. My GPS position gives me confidence, so I continue to parallel the shore without visible references for a few more minutes. With still no land in sight, I finally edge back to the left to regain visual contact. Then I press on for another kilometre, watching a blue patch overhead and to my right. Unfortunately, that spot of potential clearing is on the eastern shore, and I'm not about to cross the channel

under these conditions. I haven't seen a moving boat all afternoon, but I don't want to be hit by the first one.

The GPS shows me still south of Three-Mile Bay, but I make an uncharacteristically wise decision. I turn around. As if to punish me for such a logical choice, the sun beams down at an angle that makes visibility even worse. I'm driving right into the glare.

I follow the shoreline very slowly, pass One-Mile Bay, and angle outward to avoid the stumps along the beach just north of the Shinglemill. The long boom of logs that marks the edge of the marina pops into view. There's Joe's houseboat, *Private Dancer*, *Toot*, and the *Mugwump*.

It's a familiar sight that cheers me. And now I'll go back to town, satisfied that I tried, and sit waiting for the fog to clear.

* * * * *

That night, just after sunset, Pacific Coastal finally manages to get a Beech 1900 into Powell River. Their flight from Vancouver is along the coast in clear skies, swooping in for a landing on Runway Two-

Seven, while the far end of the runway (nearer the chuck) remains covered by fog. Margy holds a reservation on the 7 am flight the next morning, and now she has an airplane.

In the morning news, CBC radio pokes fun at Powell River. They note that the residents have been struggling with fog for days while the rest of the south coast is enjoying mostly clear skies. However, fog has now moved into Vancouver too. When we get to the airport, the airline agent announces Margy's flight as: "unlikely to land at Vancouver, unless the weather improves dramatically." The alternate is Victoria.

While Margy waits in the terminal, I walk around outside in the predawn fog and yell "Good Morning!" to Daniel through the fence as he supervises the de-icing of the Beech 1900. (Read more about Daniel, a Pacific Coastal pilot, in *Up the Airway*.) An airline worker is poised on a high stand behind the aircraft, spraying fluid on the T-tail though a tube that looks like a garden hose. Meanwhile, another fellow is tossing salt on the ramp, between the airplane's entry door and the terminal. The weather office has designated these conditions as "fog depositing ice," a wicked blend of clear ice that forms in the saturated air that is just below freezing. The same "black ice" that makes roads hazardous is even more of a problem on airfoils.

"De-icing fluid – impressive," I yell to Daniel, who comes over to the fence to talk to me.

"Hot water," he replies. "Better than nothing."

Oh, it really is a garden hose.

"You're gonna' have quite a day," I predict.

"I probably won't be home tonight," replies Daniel. "Vancouver is below minimums, according to last hour's report."

"Have fun!" I yell as Daniel goes back to supervising the spray of hot water.

Back inside the terminal, I join Margy as the call for boarding is issued. When the last passenger exits the building, the airline agent provides a few words of encouragement:

"Have a good flight, wherever you end up." Then she turns to me and adds: "Now that wasn't very nice." We both laugh.

Daniel stands by the air-stairs as the passengers climb into the airplane. Then he grabs the hose and gives the props one last spray before climbing aboard himself.

I watch the twin turboprop taxi away into the fog. The engines throttle up at the end of the runway. Then off they go.

An hour later, Margy calls me on her cell phone:

"Two guesses where I am," she kids.

"Vancouver," I reply.

"Right you are. It was quite a landing. I figured it would be a missed approach. At the last minute, I saw runway lights, felt a thump, and we were down."

I just knew Daniel would have fun today.

* * * * *

By mid-day, there is promise of clearing. Even at the ferry terminal, there is a faint brightening. So before I try going up the lake again, I drive up to the airport to try to get my Piper Arrow into the air. After an extended period of inactivity, the airplane needs a short flight to keep the engine in shape, particularly after several weeks of rain followed by extensive fog depositing ice.

When I arrive at the airport, the sky is clearing rapidly, with lots of blue to the east and overhead. The runway is still covered by fog at the west end, but conditions are improving fast. I prepare to untie the airplane and pull it out of the hangar.

Although the hangar is an open-ended T-design, it keeps the Arrow well protected from precipitation. But the covering is not immune to fog depositing ice. The fuselage and wings are covered by huge drops of water, the result of melting ice that was deposited by fog within the hangar during the cold night. The hangar keeps the Arrow out of the rain and snow, but not out of the fog.

Before I can get the ropes untied, the fog moves back in. It returns that fast. If I had taken off during the brief moments of clearing, I would not have been able to return here for landing.

This week, airplanes fail to fly, and most boats don't move. Black ice covers the highways, and everything is shrouded in fog. Ferries blast their fog horns, but move on schedule. And Powell River feels even more like an island.

◊ ◊ ◊ ◊ ◊ ◊

Chapter 4

The Head

While the Bayliner is in Powell Lake for the winter, I set a priority for making an overnight voyage to the head of Powell Lake. But that trip is delayed by storm after storm moving across coastal BC throughout the winter. Even when there is a respite of clearing behind a frontal system, it is usually too brief or the break in the weather is packed with strong northwest winds. By the time the winds die down, the next storm is inbound, bringing heavy rain and southeast winds. Although a few weather windows open, they are on weekdays, when crew boats occupy the Head's logging dock. Anchoring in the deep water at the Head (or almost anywhere on Powell Lake) is not a practical alternative.

Finally, four days before the calendar's official start of spring, a Saturday arrives with a reasonable opportunity for the trip. A weak storm moves through. We expect showery precipitation and cold temperatures, but there is little threat of strong wind. At 1 pm, it is still raining, but the boat sits loaded and ready to launch for the one-hour journey up the lake to the Head. With plenty of daylight remaining, we only need confirmation that clearing is beginning. The 4 pm marine weather report is our last check before departing; it verifies that improving conditions are already beginning in Campbell River, 50 kilometres to the west.

Margy removes the dock lines while I warm up the engine. The rain is now merely a cold drizzle, but it's enough to force us inside the Bayliner's cabin. My preferred position for driving this boat is up on the command bridge, where I have a better view of flotsam. On a day like today, with the lake near its highest level, logs float everywhere. From inside the boat's cabin, debris is difficult to see, particularly when hidden in the troughs of waves. It takes particularly adverse weather to force me to drive from inside, but this is such a day.

Motoring out of Hole in the Wall at near-idle, we S-turn through the debris field that typically accumulates in our tranquil bay. Reaching mid-channel, I finally push the throttle forward, and the Bayliner rises on-plane in rippled water. The windshield wiper and an occasional swipe of the window with a towel provide a reasonable (but still constricted) forward view. Margy boosts herself up on the port-side cushion, propping herself on her knees for the best log-spotting view out of her wiperless side of the windshield. In good conditions, this arrangement would be uncomfortable for us. Today, with our forward visibility restricted by the rain, the situation is far from adequate.

We drive like this for a few kilometres, passing Elvis Rock, now sticking out from Goat Island without the stalwart plywood image of Elvis holding his guitar. A winter storm has blasted Elvis to who-knows-where.

As we round the point, the rain eases, and visibility suddenly increases. This provides a better view from below, but it also opens the possibility of driving from above. My decision is easy – I come off-plane, slip into neutral, and up we go to the command bridge.

What a view from up here! You appreciate it even more after you've been stuck in the cabin below for awhile. Now I can clearly see floating logs in all directions, making me wonder how many unseen logs we've almost hit in the past few minutes. Even when the rain begins again, another kilometre up the lake, we stay up here. Although we're now getting soaked on the open command bridge, the improved visibility from this higher vantage point is worth the tradeoff.

When the showers increase and water begins to work its way through our jackets, I stop to wait for improvement. It doesn't take long – in just a few minutes the rain stops, and we're on our way again.

That's the end of the showers for the rest of the trip, although low clouds threaten to drop to the water's surface as fog. Just when it looks like the way ahead will be closed, we slip out into higher ceilings and improved visibility. After passing Beartooth Creek, the sun begins to break through. On again, off again, we cruise below low clouds with sunny breaks, and glassy water the rest of the way.

We divert nearer to shore to get close-up views of waterfalls plunging to the lake from mountains on both sides of our boat. Water pours down from the nearly vertical slopes – a mix of narrow streams and occasional wide veils, an amazing sight.

When we arrive at the Head, no boats are parked at the logging dock. We decide to continue another kilometre north to the river's inlet.

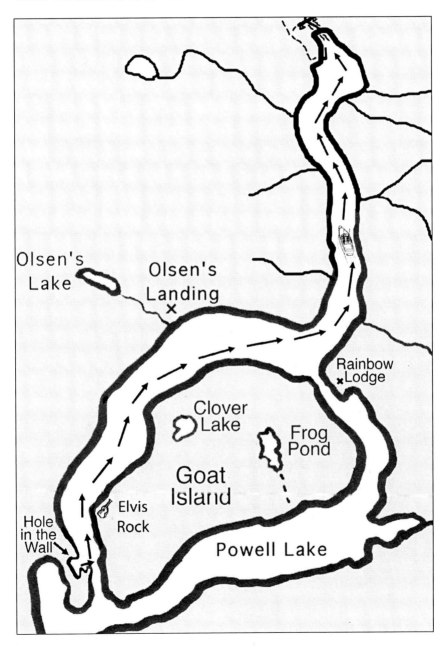

Here churning water pours down out of Powell River, augmented by its upstream merger with Daniels River. Cascades flow below the bridge that crosses here, pounding over huge slabs of granite. In turbulent swirls, we reverse course. I use a touch of power to propel the Bayliner out of the slithering current. Then we tie-up at the logging dock.

As we secure the boat, patches of blue sky ride over the towering mountains, changing into pockets of pink as evening approaches. The feeling that the Head is a lake unto itself is enhanced as the sun drops towards the tall peaks to the west, casting streams of light on the opposite shore. The Head is surrounded by tree-shrouded mountains dropping down into the water. I feel like we're in the mouth of a giant crater – a caldera full of water.

There's still lots of light left for a short hike, so Margy and I walk along the dirt road through the empty logging camp. At the bridge over the river, in a quickly-passing shower, we look down on the tumbling torrent of water pouring into Powell Lake. Margy snaps a photo of me through a rain-spotted lens.

On the way back to the boat, it stops raining. We hike contentedly, knowing we have this time to ourselves in a scenic spot that few people have visited. Except for those who come here to log, few recreational boaters visit the Head. We feel privileged to be here on this spring-like evening, ushering out winter in a very special way.

* * * * *

The next morning, we are awake and ready to go by 9 am. When it is time to cast off from the dock, I sit on the command bridge, still warming up the engine. I don't want to let go of our dock lines until I'm sure the engine is ready to shift into gear without stalling. It's a good engine, but it demands a slow warm-up, so I ask Margy to stay on the dock, holding the last line while the engine settles in.

The Bayliner begins to drift outward in the wind. Margy has a firm grasp on the stern line, but the untied bow is slipping outward. Another brief gust pushes the bow out farther, and suddenly the boat is at a 45-degree angle to the dock. With a handrail blocking the corner of the stern, the entry to the aft deck (just forward of the rail) is now a big step. If Margy waits any longer, it will be too late.

"Hop in!" I yell.

I watch Margy throw the line over the handrail. She grabs the rail, but doesn't step aboard. The stern is already too far from the dock for her comfort. Margy is the first to admit a lack of surefootedness in tight situations, and there is no need to stretch her limits. So I offer her an alternative.

"Just let go," I say. "I'll swing around and come back to the dock to pick you up."

As if to contradict my suggestion, and maybe to self-test her own sense of confidence in this tight situation, Margy decides to go for it. From the command bridge, I watch her step onto the transom-mounted swim grid just as the stern separates from the dock. The wind pushes us out quickly, but now she is committed and aboard the boat – sort of. The handrail blocks her access to the aft deck, but she hangs onto it. She balances herself precariously on the swim grid, wedged between the rail and the dinghy that blocks entry over the transom.

"I'll take you back to the dock, and you can jump off."

My suggestion seems like the simplest solution, since I can swing around quickly and let her step off onto the dock. But she isn't buying it. I look down at her, and she nods *No*. It isn't a defiant *No*. Instead, it's a clear indication she is frightened and wants to be completely aboard, right now. She scoots down a bit, clinging to the rail with a two-handed death grip.

I leave the engine idling in neutral and rush down the stairs from the command bridge. I immediately offer Margy my hand, hoping to help her climb over the rail and onto the aft deck. But she isn't about to let go of the rail with either hand. I look into her eyes and see fear. She is precariously balanced on the edge of the swim grid, only a metre from safety on the aft deck but kilometres from her own sense of security.

"Give me your hand. I'll help you over the rail."

Her eyes say *No*.

She scrunches down on her haunches and crawls on her knees along the swim grid, under the dinghy, and to the center of transom where there is a narrow opening under the handrail. She tries to squeeze through, but the opening below the dinghy is too small. I help her remove her jacket and life vest, so she can crawl through and onto the aft deck. She ends up in a ball on the deck, but she is safe and finally fully aboard.

We both begin to laugh at the absurdity of her entry to the boat.

"I'm aboard now," Margy laughs.

"So I see. Are we finally ready to go?"

"I think so," she replies. "I'm just glad you didn't get a picture of this."

She's right. I missed a golden opportunity.

Chapter 5

Turf It

John manages to drive his Suzuki Samurai to Theodosia Valley, then all the way to Hole in the Wall for a visit. After a grueling journey over mountain trails, which includes dealing with a flat tire, he finally maneuvers the jeep-like vehicle down to Cabin Number 2.

This Suzuki is not really a Samurai (which was built the following year), but it has all of the characteristics of the better-known model. It sports a small profile (one of the original SUVs) and a notorious record for rollover accidents. Its high center of gravity earned it a reputation that finally killed the product line.

John's Samurai (we call it "The Jeep") has been modified with a hefty roll bar, a permanently open top, and a flat cargo area where the rear seat once resided. The Jeep displays a solid structure with lots of stainless-steel, and John has added new brakes and an overhauled exhaust system. Although the old engine is in good condition, it sounds like a sewing machine and is cranked by a marginal battery that requires constant attention.

The Jeep demands a wider trail than a quad, but it provides us with (cramped) onboard space for four. On a typical ride, John and Margy ride up front in luxury, while Bro and I argue over minimal space in the rear. With efficient loading, we can carry a chainsaw, tools, shovel, food, and our personal gear.

On the trip to the cabin from Theodosia Valley, Jim joined John in the Suzuki, while John's brother, Dave, followed them on his quad. Along several stretches of Heather Main, Dave had to put all of his weight on one side of the Jeep (outboard ballast) to allow John to get down some of the steeper slopes without tipping over.

When John arrived with the Suzuki, it was pretty much a matter of ramming the vehicle through an overgrown trail that leads from the

logging road to a makeshift parking area above Cabin Number 2. The last part of the journey on the short trail was possible only with the help of several friends who were waiting for him at the cabin. Together they pushed and even lifted the Jeep down the steepest switchbacks.

Now the latest project for John and me is to improve the trail from the cabin to the logging road. Old dirt mains, inactive but usable, run all over the region, creating a huge interconnected web, but first we need a clear route out to the nearest road.

The first day of trail building is a killer, since we have to move a lot of dirt. We'll also need to move some big boulders, a major part of the job. In six hours of hard work, we progress 20 metres by using a pick, shovel, and chainsaw. I'm exhausted.

The next day, things move a bit quicker, as we advance out of the trees and into the bush. The route to be renovated is a half kilometre of switchbacks that leads to the old logging road. Much remains to be done, but there are visible signs of progress.

One of the keys to our slow but steady pace is a "turfer," a hand-winch that can pull almost anything out of the way and haul even the largest fallen log from the trail.

"I don't get it," I remark to John. "Why is it called a 'turfer' rather than a winch?"

"Really the same thing," he replies. "It pulls almost anything out of the way – you turf it. Yank it and throw it aside."

"Turf it?"

"Sure. Throw it away. Turf it."

I look on the side of the winch. Its engraved plate says: *Tirfmaster – Toronto – 1500 pounds*. Later, I look it up in the dictionary.

Turf (verb – British slang): force someone or something to leave a position or location ("They were turfed off the bus.")

To move a particularly large dead stump that juts into the trail, we connect the turfer to a snatch block. The block's pulley allows us to reverse the direction of the steel cable, doubling the already high torque we produce when we pump the winch handle. The turfer and snatch block sit between the stump and a nearby anchor tree. A rope extends out each end of the turfer to a choker cable that is attached to the stump in one direction and to the anchor tree on the opposite side. The mechanical advantage of this simple system allows us to move almost anything with up to 3000 pounds of pulling power.

* * * * *

A few days after our trail construction, Margy and I take our tin boat across the bay to Cabin Number 2. We climb up the cliff to the Jeep's parking spot, where we plan to surprise John by cleaning out his turnaround spot. We move dirt to build up the width on the downhill side of the parking area. We dig, cut mid-trail snags with my chainsaw (oops – sparks), and shovel dirt into buckets for hauling to the low side of the trail. After a few hours of this, we are totally exhausted.

"Visualize this," I say to Margy. "Think about how you feel right now, and then imagine trail building as quad riders know it."

We know about a major trail building project that John and his friends have been working on during the past few weeks near Ice Lake. They work persistently in a very challenging environment, often in the rain.

"It's awfully hard work," acknowledges Margy. "And they work at it a lot harder than we have today."

"Pushing dirt here for just a few hours, it's easy to put it in perspective," I add. "After working like this, those guys stop for a short lunch break and then go back at it for another two or three hours. Then they face a long hike out, followed by a ride on quads 30 klicks back to their trucks. After that, they still have to load their quads into their trucks, drive home, and unload. That's trail building."

As we work near the Jeep, I encounter an extensive ash layer 10 centimetres below the surface. It's a natural occurring geological layer that's probably several thousand years old, maybe even older. I've found this ash when clearing debris with John in other parts of the trail. In this spot, the ash is extensive, probably evidence of an old forest fire in the area.

I also find rocks that resemble sea-like limestone. I put a few small chunks in my backpack for further study back at the cabin.

John thinks water from upper Powell Lake flowed through this now-elevated area in an ancient wide river that may have included (or bypassed) First Narrows. There's a lot of evidence of water erosion on the cliffs throughout this area. It's a region of known uplift as the land rebounded after the retreat of an ancient ice sheet. The same ice-age glacier dug out the fjord that became Powell Lake. Maybe this spot was the original First Narrows of the lower lake, where rushing water tumbled southward. Today, it's a short hop to the lower lake through the trees at the back of John's bay.

* * * * *

Back at our cabin, I smash open one of the rocks. I find what looks like many tiny fossils. A hand magnifying glass allows me to zoom in on the elusive marks. I wouldn't be surprised to find a perfectly preserved Trilobite, but instead find many fossilized shell-like structures. Of course, shelled organisms exist on land (snails), but I imagine these marks to be remnants of underwater life. I use the top of a firewood splitting stump to pulverize the rock with my hammer. I save a few fragments that contain what looks to me like small fossil shells.

I show the rock fragments to Margy. Her eyes are better than mine, so she should be able to confirm my suspicions. Using the magnifying lens, she surmises they are merely routine conglomerates in the rock.

But my imagination is convinced these are fossils. No matter how many times I examine the specimens, I see the same shells.

Later I show the rocks to John. He doesn't need the magnifier to conclude these are not fossils. Regardless, I keep the rocks on a shelf in the cabin as proof of what I consider ancient sea life.

* * * * *

The winter of 2006-07 is the windiest season in my seven years in Powell River. Even the locals are amazed by the severity of these winter storms. Nearly every week, wind velocities approach 100 kilometres per hour, with the worst of it hitting the coast in December, rather than in the traditionally windy and wild November.

Another unusual aspect of this winter includes the accumulation of considerable snow. A major snowstorm batters the south coast in late November, fortunately without any significant winds. The winds come a month late; the snow a month early. It's a November winter wonderland at Hole in the Wall. Fifteen centimetres of snow fall in two days, with plenty to build a snowman on the deck of our cabin.

When I return to the States for Christmas, John gives me regular telephone updates regarding the storms. Winds pound Hole in the Wall in a relentless series of back-to-back blasts. My cabin receives more damage in a few weeks than in my previous years on the lake.

Two shore-to-cabin cables break, the chimney departs the cabin, and the barbecue grill is swept from the deck. John breaks the news by explaining his shock (and amusement) when he walked around the corner of the cabin and found only the legs of the barbecue sticking up from the deck. The entire top portion was tossed into the lake. John decides to leave the bottom structure for me to see. I used this trusty barbecue nearly every day on the float, so it seems only appropriate that we have a "Will-it-float?" ceremony upon my return.

* * * * *

In early January, Margy and I fly from Bellingham to Powell River in our Piper Arrow. It's the first day of decent flying weather since Christmas. The U.S. Pacific Northwest, like coastal BC, is recovering from a stormy December that has left communities near Seattle without power for weeks.

What starts out as a partly sunny day in Bellingham, with a forecast for an easy flight to Powell River, becomes a major struggle. Halfway to Victoria, over the San Juan Islands, a storm cell appears to our right. It hangs ominously over the southern portion of the Strait of Georgia. We divert southward towards downtown Victoria. With the freezing level at 3000 feet, it's prudent to remain under visual flight rules (VFR), deviating as necessary to stay out of the icing conditions within the clouds. With the concurrence of air traffic control, we maneuver between clouds, dropping to 2000 feet over Victoria Airport, then flying below the increasingly threatening overcast.

We slip along the coast of Vancouver Island towards Nanaimo, our required Customs stop. It's a battle the entire way – around, below, and then over the cumulus. The clouds finally end a few miles south of Nanaimo, and we begin a screaming descent from 8000 feet to land under nearly-clear skies.

From Nanaimo, it's fair weather all the way to Powell River, with a surprise over Texada Island. The ground is covered by fresh snow from a quick but fierce morning storm that wasn't in the forecast. We make it into Powell River without further incident (1.9 hours from Bellingham, nearly double the normal flight time). That night, another wintery blast moves in. Pounding rain and blustery winds keep us in town for the next two days.

After the latest storm abates, we finally arrive at Hole in the Wall. I step out of the boat into the remains of a disaster area. Wood is floating everywhere – logs of all sizes are rammed against the breakwater and the cabin, and thousands of tiny chunks drift aimlessly. It will be enough firewood to last a month.

The deck is full of the evidence of strong winds during our absence. The barbecue base stands proudly under the porch roof, old broken steel cables are scattered on the deck and shore, and remnants of John's work are everywhere. Like a car mechanic who shows you old parts before they're discarded, John likes to display the destroyed components. He knows I have full trust in his work, but he figures I can learn from this. He's right – I like to see the damaged mechanisms. But in this case the amount of destruction is so extensive that metal and wood debris are everywhere. It looks like a war zone.

The cabin now sports several new shoreline cables with a modified tether system that John feels will weather the storms better. The new cables (seven-eighth-inch in diameter) are joined halfway to the granite cliff by old tires. The tires take up some of the stress, forming mid-cable shock absorbers. It's an ingenious design that John has invented as a solution for absorbing the enormous forces placed on the cables and the anchor bolts embedded in the cliff. From the deck, I see the tires submerged a metre below the surface at the mid-point of the new cables. (During the next storm, I will stand on the deck as the cabin swings outward from shore, watching the tires rise to the surface, flex slightly, and do their job to bring us to a smooth halt. With this modification, the cabin rides with much more stability in high winds. John is, in my opinion, the world's most accomplished aquatic engineer.)

Adding to today's clutter on the cabin deck is an old wooden boat that lies damaged beyond repair. John pulled the beat-up "treasure" onto our deck when it washed up against the cabin in a recent storm. Its bottom is ripped open, but John figures I can use it as a giant planter.

Instead, I eventually lash it to the rear deck, where it serves admirably as a huge container for collected scraps of kindling – a firewood boat.

The new chimney is also improved in design, with heavier metal straps connecting it to the roof. One of the larger fasteners is a bracket John cannibalized from the remnants of the base of the destroyed barbecue. He's an expert at recycling even the most worthless-looking hardware. Months later, while working on the porch roof, I come across the chimney bracket, clearly labeled *MasterChef.*

* * * * *

John's visits to Hole in the Wall are always the highlight of my day. They are sometimes also a trying experience.

Whenever I see John's boat pop around the headlands of First Narrows, there is a sense of excitement. Sometimes he zooms around the corner. At other times he plods slowly into the Hole, towing some prized object found floating during his journey up the lake.

On this particular day, I know his visit will be physically demanding. Today has been designated as a cleanup day in John's back bay. I'm pleased I can help him, considering all the hard work he constantly expends on projects for me. But I also know it will be exhausting. John never tackles a project timidly.

Two ravens orbit overhead, their huge wings beating the air with a hefty whoosh-whoosh. It's an early-warning-signal that John is approaching. These birds know John and Bro, and they lay in wait. Sure, it sounds ridiculous, but these ravens follow John and Bro around when they are in the Hole. Unfortunately, they are after food rather than friendship. John does not provide them with food graciously.

Maybe these birds associate a food source with Bro, since it is often his dog food that they steal. These scoundrels also dig into John's backpack for sandwiches and cookies. Just yesterday, a raven greeted John and Bro by swooping down to my cabin and perching on the top of the Campion. Bro ran in circles on the deck, barking like a madman. The trickster knew he was safe on top of the boat, so he just sat there, tormenting the poor dog. Then the raven flew only a few metres to the top of John's boat, teasing Bro even further.

That afternoon, while John was in my cabin, a raven entered John's boat. The bird skulked under the canvas to the front seat, dug into a zippered backpack, and stole an unopened tin can containing Brody's sardines. There was indisputable evidence – the can was missing from the now unzipped backpack.

"Don't believe me? Take a look at that," taunted John, as he pointed at the top of the nearby cliff.

Two ravens scrambled over the top of the cliff, a silver can tumbling back and forth over the rocks. I grabbed my binoculars, focusing just in time to verify it was indeed a rectangular sardine can. These scoundrels are sneaky, persistent, and absolutely intent on their targeted victims – John and Bro.

With the ravens now circling overhead, it is no surprise when John arrives a few minutes later via the slow route, rounding the point close to shore with a large piece of flotsam in tow.

"I couldn't pass it up," announces John. "It was just floating around by Cassiar Island, waiting for me."

He attaches the ragged wooden structure to the inside of my breakwater, to be stored for eventual redistribution to Cabin Number 2.

"What is it?" I ask.

"Part of a walkway, blown away in one of the latest storms," he states matter-of-factly. "Maybe someone will claim it, but it's hard to say where it came from."

My breakwater already has two other large logs that John has temporarily stored here, broken off from cabin booms during recent storms. They float on ropes from my transition float, for eventual storage at one of John's cabins, unless claimed by the original owners. They have no real purpose, but they are navigational hazards on the lake, so John has towed them here. He may eventually find a use for them. John discards nothing, which results in quite a collection of wood at Cabins Number 1 and Number 2.

High water levels, coinciding with recent wind storms, have caused breakwater logs and cabin structures to break loose all over the lake. John collects the more valuable flotsam, sometimes securing it to the outside of his breakwater at one of his cabins, in case someone wants to claim it. I refer to it as "The 14-Day Rule." If an item is not claimed within two weeks, it's fair game for use elsewhere. But John exceeds the "14-Day Rule" on the most valuable items, leaving them subject to claim almost indefinitely.

Currently, a huge chunk of someone's breakwater that drifted free is now tethered to the outside of John's breakwater at Number 2, where it can easily be seen and claimed. A huge 500-pound white propane tank floats half-submerged in his back bay, and John has pulled numerous 55-gallon blue barrels (used for cabin flotation) from the open water in various locations on the lake.

Today, after traveling up the lake, John reports an entire cabin is floating mid-channel near One-Mile Bay. He decided the cabin was outside the scope of the "14-Day Rule," so he left it to drift, eventually to be claimed by its owner. A free-floating cabin is not the norm. But this is not a normal winter.

In preparation for today's project, we remove tools and equipment from John's boat and transfer them to my tin boat. With its metal hull, low-profile outboard motor, and bullet-proof prop, we'll be able to get in closer to shore. We load two turfer hand-winches with their bulky cables, piles of heavy rope, chains, log staples, shackles, choke cables, snatch blocks, and a big, black dog. Then we're off to Number 2 to try to extract some of the residue that has been pushed into John's back bay during a recent storm. Much of it is now firmly lodged on the shore due to receding lake levels. John wants to restore his bay to the beautiful natural setting that it should be. This will be a task that takes a lot of muscle and considerable sweat on this freezing day. It's the ultimate example of going to war with Mother Nature, and it's pretty obvious who will come out ahead. But maybe we can win one small battle.

Behind Number 2, I get my first close look at the trees that have been blown down during a recent fierce storm. The wind that destroyed over 30 trees must have been immense. To me, the swath of destruction looks like a tornado or a severe microburst from a thunderstorm. In fact, it could have been exactly that, a vicious wind during the passage of a highly unstable cold front. John prefers to refer to it as a "hurricane," but there were no humans here to document the powerful blast as it occurred. Many of the trees were completely uprooted, others brutally snapped off. Twisted remains are everywhere.

We work for two hours, wearing our bodies ragged as we clean up the back bay. By forestry regulations, the fallen trees on the beach are off-limits, but we manage to clean up much of the floating residue. John tows a small raft into position to mount the turfer, cabled to a

nearby half-submerged stump, allowing us to untangle some of the jammed logs.

With its new backdrop of fallen trees, this bay will never be the same, but it is a bit more orderly now. I look to the south through the broken barricade that once protected this bay, an area now open to

storms. Notorious southeast winds will blow unrestricted into Hole in the Wall for the first time in recent history. About 15 years ago, this area was logged extensively, but no trees were taken within 50 feet of shore. That was supposed to be enough to protect the shoreline. In reality, such thin lines of trees usually don't last long. With the primary forest gone, the remaining trees are unprotected from the wind. Here in John's back bay, the thin timber barricade has been breached permanently.

Logging is an important part of the local economy. But as John would say: "Whose forests are these anyway?" The thin line of shoreline trees is enough to aggravate his low opinion of current logging practices. It doesn't help that U.S. companies do some of the logging, and much of the lumber is shipped to the States.

The prolonged softwood export issue, which affects most of the logging operations in this region, makes matters even worse for British Columbia logging companies. Logs that make it across the border to the States are exempt from the fair trade protection provided for other exports, reducing the profit for BC loggers. It's a sore issue that few locals understand, except to know that their logs are not properly priced on the open market. If you need a topic to start an argument, logging will do it!

Today's project has been a demanding exercise, but John's back bay is looking less cluttered now. I question whether all of this has been worth the effort. It seems to have made but a dent in the landscape.

But when I see the grin on John's face, I know the answer. To match wits with the wrath of Mother Nature may seem futile, but John is justifiably pleased about winning a minor battle. As for me, I sleep well that night, knowing that I have contributed to John's feeling of having accomplished something worthwhile.

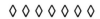

Chapter 6

Beachcombing Goat

While I stand at the back of Margy's truck pumping gas, John pulls in next to us, grabs a cruise-a-day container from the back of his truck, and uses the marine pump to fill it up. We smile at each other, possibly because there is nothing that needs to be said. Powell River is a small town in many respects, and seems to be even smaller at times like this. For a resident of Los Angeles, it's close to shocking.

John and I met only half an hour ago near the airport, where we talked truck-to-truck in a store parking lot. After our brief meeting, we agreed to meet at my cabin later in the afternoon. Now here we are at adjacent pumps in a gas station filling up trucks and gas cans. It's an amazing coincidence. But this happens so often that it seems a bit spooky.

Margy and I leave the station, knowing that John still needs to go inside to pay for his gas. We drive directly to the Shinglemill. As we pull into the marina, I'm dumbfounded to find John already parked and on the dock. He took the shore route, and we took the inland route. The difference in distance is not significant, but he has arrived first once again. Wherever I go, he always gets there first. It's uncanny.

John and Bro make several trips to their boat, loading tools and materials for a fix-it project at my cabin, while Margy and I head to our boat with our backpacks and a few bags from Canadian Tire.

"See you later," I say to John as he makes one more trip back to his truck while we continue along the ramp to our Campion.

"You bet. Don't let all these tools fool you. I'm just bringing them in case I get bored. The swim ladder might not get fixed today."

"Of course," I reply. "It's not a priority."

After yesterday's long stint of trail building, John is dragging today. But, as always, he beats me everywhere. Our primary reason for meeting up the lake at my cabin is to investigate a float that is for sale at Rainbow Lodge. Well, it's not exactly on the market, but everything has a price. The lodge might consider selling the old float, since it has become an eyesore. And John needs float logs to build a new cabin. He hasn't had any luck finding the right cedar logs in the past few months, so making an offer on this old float is a reasonable consideration.

I back the Campion from the dock finger, looking behind me to assure adequate clearance. There sits John in his Hourston, already out of his boat slip and waiting for me to clear the area. How does he do that so fast?

Outside the Shinglemill breakwater, I throttle up and point the bow directly at Cassiar Island. Normally, I would follow the east shore, past John's Number 4 and Number 1 cabins, just to check that everything looks secure. But today John will take care of that, so I take the shortcut. This route is not wise when the lake is rough, but today the water is nearly calm.

Looking behind me, I see the Hourston arc towards the east shore, riding in distant formation with our boat, and then splitting off to the right. I'll actually beat him to my cabin today, but that's only because he makes two stops along the way.

* * * * *

"Let's get going, in case it rains," says John a few minutes after docking at Cabin Number 3.

Bro is charging around the cabin deck, checking things out at his normal frenzied pace. Whenever he arrives at a destination, however temporary, he goes into his high-speed mode of exploring and sniffing. He knows this cabin well and feels at home here, but still the frantic dance.

"We're ready," I reply. "I'll bring a can of gas, just in case."

"Never can have too much," says John. "Do you want to go up past Olsen's or back around through First Narrows?"

"I assume Olsen's is quicker, but either is fine. Maybe we should go one way and return the other, all the way around Goat Island."

"Sure!" says John.

Since it's my boat and my gas today, he wouldn't have suggested the complete circuit. But he's quick to agree to a trip that promises variety.

In the Campion, John plops down in the front passenger seat. I notice he doesn't offer to ride in back, but I'm surprised he doesn't automatically take the helm. He always drives everywhere we go. I like it that way, he likes it that way, and there is no other way. His courtesy today draws a shrug from me, as I point to the right seat.

"Okay," he says. "If you insist."

Margy is last aboard, but I guide her towards the front seat. On the boat, I enjoy wandering around, from bow to stern. Today, my seat is in the rear. Bro slips into the bow and takes a position that will allow him to catch the wind. He isn't big on riding in most boats, but he tolerates the Campion with its bowrider design.

John cranks the engine, and we're off. We wave to Jess on his tiny float ("8 by 10, just like a picture"), and power up as soon as we are past. Then it's out of the Hole and left towards Elvis Rock.

As I sit (for the time being) behind Margy, John leans back and yells something I can't understand. I pull my ear defenders off: "What?"

"Maybe we should check out that log at Olsen's Landing," yells John.

Olsen's is a bit out of our way, and John is always conscious of using someone else's gas.

"Sure," I reply.

John smiles and points the bow slightly to the left towards the log dump. But halfway across the channel, Margy yells something at John and points to the right. John shakes his head ("*Yes*") and veers towards the eastern side of the lake. Not surprisingly, the destination is a huge stump that floats about 100 metres from the shore. We swing around a bobbing trunk that sprouts a small tree and a host of other plants. We pause for a few moments, admiring the stump's classic lines.

"That would look good at our cabin," says Margy.

"Sure would," answers John.

But it's understood by all of us that it's a long tow back to Hole in the Wall. Still, it's nice to picture the stump sitting alongside our breakwater. We all love stumps, particularly ones with elegant designs like this.

John loops the Campion back across our own wake (*tha-thump*) and again points the boat at Olsen's Landing on the opposite shore. As we cross the channel, I slide under the walk-through windshield (no need to open it) and out into the bow. Battered by the cool but not uncomfortable wind, I take a seat with Bro, riding with my legs propped up on the front rail.

Bro seems calm in the bowrider, but he still pants and drools as he often does when he gets nervous. I'm downwind of him, so I decide to shift my position after a few drops of Bro's slobber hit my shirt.

As we approach Olsen's Landing, John slows to idle, and I move full-forward to lie on my back, with my head on the point of the bow, lounging with Bro in the now-gentle breeze.

A barge full of shake blocks, already on pallets, rests against the shore, and a huge log bobs nearby, two-thirds of it submerged in the water. John has been watching this log for months.

"It's almost ready," says John. "Just needs a little more water before it comes loose."

The lake level has been coming up at a fairly rapid pace in recent weeks, setting loose tons of wood from the shore. As June marches onward, Powell Lake is increasingly covered with prop-breaking obstacles.

"It looks old, almost rotten," I note. "But it must not be, if you're interested."

"It's old all right, but solid. A skookum log."

Skookum it is. Big – nearly 5 feet in diameter and almost 100 feet long.

After admiring the log, John backs out of the area and heads directly towards Second Narrows, a tricky spot to navigate, unless you're familiar with it. John weaves through the entrance and around the corner towards Rainbow Lodge, a majestic place originally used as a retreat for managers of the town's paper mill.

We dock near Rainbow Lodge, at the old float that is sort-of for sale. The float is about 25 metres long, with a dilapidated long-and-skinny cabin sitting on top of it.

I'm first out of the boat, followed closely by Bro. On my first step onto the deck, my foot caves through a rotten cedar plank, but I recover before my leg falls all the way down into the float structure. I regain my balance and step back onto the deck. If I'd looked closer, I would have seen that the old boards include many deteriorated sections that require caution when walking.

We carefully walk the deck, from one end to other, stepping inside the back room of the cabin, which is unlocked. The building itself is large for a float cabin, and the cedar foundation is particularly huge. Big is good for John's needs, but the logs are very old. They are of substantial size, but all are waterlogged with age, riding only a few inches above the water.

"I don't think it will work," says John. "You can't tell how high the float will ride with the cabin removed until you tear it down. But I don't think the logs would come up very much."

We lean over the side, and he shows me how logs have been added below the original float to bring the waterlogged logs upward. It's a principal similar to the use of air-filled barrels under today's cabins. In decades past, logs themselves provided the only flotation. It's hard to imagine how you could shove such huge logs under an existing float.

We pace off the dimensions. John leans over the float at one edge and peers underneath. Then he walks back to a broken section of decking, kneels down, and looks through the smashed planks. He mulls over the situation.

"The float would have to be taken completely apart, right down to the separate logs. Maybe I could reuse some of the logs, but it would be a lot of work, no matter how you look at it."

"None of the cabin could be used?" I ask.

"No, we'd rip it down. Or maybe burn it."

"Burn it down? Right on the float?"

"Sure. We'd have to be careful, but it could be done safely. It'd make quite a sight."

"Man, I'd like to see that! But wouldn't it burn up the float too."

"No, that's really not a problem. Even if most of the old deck burned, the logs in the water would be barely charred. Talk about wet wood – those logs are really soaked."

It'd be worth buying the float just to watch the fire.

While John inspects things further, I retrieve a fishing pole from the Campion and try a few casts. My lure attracts no bites, though I'm fishing in a spot that certainly looks like trout territory.

"I bet there are goats up there," says John, returning to the boat. "In fact, I think I see one near that ridge."

He points towards a rocky area near the top of Goat Island, and then uses binoculars to zoom in.

"One just jumped down to a lower ledge," he says. "And there's another one!"

He's excited about his find, but I'm pessimistic regarding seeing these goats. It will likely be another embarrassing attempt to see what John sees – a physical impossibility. When John hands me the binoculars, I'm prepared for disappointment.

"Try just to the right of that largest patch of snow, about halfway between that spot and the first line of trees in the rocky area. I can barely make them out myself, but there are two goats there."

Oh, great. John can barely see goats in the binoculars. The hope for me is near zero. I scan the rocky area and find no goats. This is the same game we've played together many times. I call it: "John sees goats. I see nothing." It gets embarassing after a while.

"Look for movement," says John.

I've been known to tell John I see goats, even when I don't, just so I won't disappoint him. But today I'm honest.

"I don't see them," I say.

"There should be some up there too," says John as he turns and scans the steep mountain cliffs behind Rainbow Lodge with his naked eyes.

"Oh, there's one!" he yells. "And another one! They're really moving around, and easy to spot."

I point my binoculars at the cliffs behind the lodge, and John guides me to the location.

"Go up that ravine until you find a good-sized cave in a wide-open rocky area, then to the left a bit, and then up to the first row of trees…"

"I see one!" I yell.

In the binoculars I detect a whitish-yellow blob, and it's definitely moving. Now I even see the goat jumping to another ledge. We spend a few more minutes watching several goats move around on the cliffs. One particular blob seems to be moving around just for me, keeping out of the trees and changing direction erratically. And big enough so I don't have to fabricate a little white lie.

* * * * *

Before leaving Rainbow Lodge, we discuss whether there is any way this float will work for John's cabin-building project. It's probably a dead end idea, but he might make an offer to haul it off, if there are no additional costs involved. If there is to be a bonfire, I don't want to miss it.

Leaving the bay, we continue southward to complete our circumnavigation of Goat Island. In only a few minutes, John spots a spectacular waterfall plunging off a cliff to our left. He maneuvers the boat toward the spot, and we stop only a few metres from the falls. We gaze upward in awe, watching the water cascade downward towards us. As the boat drifts into the roiling swirls near the falls, water sprays over us in a refreshing (cold!) mist.

We pull away from the falls, and I look back to notice a higher waterfall near the very top of the mountain ridge. This high-altitude stream of water is what feeds the falls on the lower cliff. I motion back toward the high stream of water, and John and Margy turn to look at

it. John gives me a smile. This lake is supernatural, and we all know it.

From the falls, we cross to the Goat Island side and skim along the shore, hunting for logs, stumps, and anything unusual in the water. What is of interest to John is varied and difficult to define. He's a beachcomber in the true sense of the word. He finds use for things

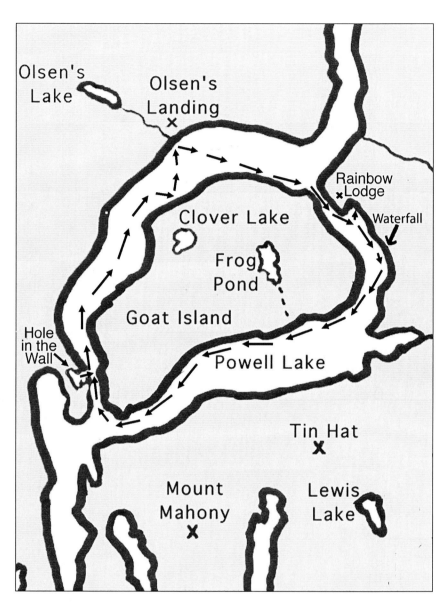

he discovers drifting on the lake and against its shores. Often he just wants to see what he can find, and then leaves it in place.

As we cruise along the shore, I scan the mountainous terrain of Goat Island, looking for bears. We pass a clearing that would be ideal for them during early June, an appropriate place to see a big mama bear and her new cubs. Several logging slashes get my attention. It would be fun to spot a bear here and stop to observe it closely. There are few places safer to be when it comes to bears than in a boat. I look and look, but I see no animals.

We glide past float cabins, admiring some, scowling at the design or condition of others. John maneuvers the boat precisely around flotsam that is everywhere on the lake today.

We cruise past the cabins owned by our friends, Danny and then Bob, but neither has a boat tied up today, so we continue on without slowing. Then we navigate through First Narrows, into Hole in the Wall, and back to Cabin Number 3.

While I fix dinner, John, Margy, and Bro launch the tin boat for one final bout of beachcombing, local style. John maneuvers the boat through the bay of Cabin Number 2, while Margy pulls wood aboard that has recently washed out from John's firewood storage area.

They also comb the back of the Hole, looking for stray logs, and return to the cabin with a few chunks of extra firewood and a flat-looking board.

"Perfect for a bench seat on your cliff," says John. "It's nice and flat on one side and rounded just a bit on the other. You can use two cutoff stumps for legs, and you'll have a seat with a view."

As I finish preparations for dinner, John uses the tools he has brought to repair our swim ladder. He fires up my gas generator to provide electrical power for his hefty drill, and uses rusty-looking large screws and spikes to secure the rungs and rails – hardware he has salvaged from old wood on the lake. Then he aligns the completed ladder at the edge of the deck, positions the final spikes a few inches below the waterline, and uses a sledgehammer to drive them home.

Driving spikes with a sledge underwater is a sight to see. It creates quite a splash. This is a typical John-engineered project that employs elements of basic design, recycled materials, and brute force. Beachcombers are a rare breed in this modern world. But they know how to construct and repair almost anything, with almost nothing.

Chapter 7

The Junco Wars

Everything is late this spring, even the birds. In early March, the tree swallows have not yet arrived from their winter homes in the south. I want to be ready this year, avoiding a repeat of the previous spring when I stuffed wooden blocks above the porch roof beam in a futile attempt to prevent birds from nesting there. I want the birds nearby, just not that close. The disturbance of their nests and the rearing of their babies must be avoided. Last year, every time I stepped out onto the porch, I was greeted by the birds' angry chatter – an octave above the normal twitter of tree swallows: "We were here first!"

I want the birds to nest comfortably nearby, where I can watch their swooping flight patterns over Hole in the Wall. Although swallows avoid flying over large bodies of water (during migration, they fly around rather than over large lakes), I've spent hours-on-end watching them swoop low over the Hole in their continuous hunt for insects. Down and around, and then upward in endless aerobatics (*Up the Lake*, Chapter 9).

I want to encourage their nesting nearby. Birdhouses are a common sight on Powell Lake, often placed on stumps that project up out of the water. Loggers and local residents of Powell Lake build them, often hung far away from cabins.

John explains that swallow houses should be hung in locations where the birds feel safe from predators, so cliffs and high stumps make excellent locations. There are no protruding stumps near Cabin Number 3, but steep cliffs drop into the water right next to our cabin. Maybe we can entice the arriving swallows to try something better than nesting under the eaves of my roof.

Another seemingly good location for a birdhouse would be on the wall of the cabin shed, which overhangs the water. A post on the floating garden already holds ducky ornaments in Christmas tree fashion, so that might also be a promising location.

John's expertise will be needed, but he is quick to respond. He loves birds, with the exception of the ravens that periodically ravage the contents of his boat and Bro's stash of dog food.

John installs five birdhouses, three on the shed, one on the top of the floating garden post, and one on the cliff. The cliff-mounted birdhouse requires drilling into the granite to secure a metre-high wooden pole. Just getting to the site necessitates a bit of rock climbing. It's a good challenge for John's engineering mind.

With the delay in spring's arrival, swallows have not yet arrived in the Hole. But five brand new birdhouses stand ready. Meanwhile, it's time to plant the floating garden, as well as the small upper garden above the cliff. Peat, manure, and slug bait are ready to be added to the soil. Slugs have not yet appeared, but they are a problem every year. Nematodes and grubs are also prevalent in the soil, but we can't find a non-toxic way to combat these garden pests, so we decide to live with them. Now all that is needed is a short stretch of good weather to work the soil, let it sit for a few days, and then plant the seeds. But waiting for the rain to end seems to take forever.

We are also concerned about a bigger critter that has left his calling card of tattered plant tops in the garden. Since the garden floats against the breakwater at night, it's possible that a land animal has taken up residence when the garden was brought in close for tending. A bushy-tailed woodrat (packrat) is the likely culprit.

In mid-March, the sun breaks through off-and-on for a full day. The topsoil dries quickly, and the next day is full of sunny breaks. Margy and I work peat and manure into the dirt. Two days later, with only intermittent showers, we transplant bare-root strawberries to replace those killed by the grubs. We also plant potatoes, and asparagus, along with a variety of seeds for onions, lettuce, carrots, spinach, and a few flowers.

I build rough planter boxes to sit in cavities in a floating stump that is tethered to our breakwater. Old boards and a few nails are enough to enclose opportune areas for potting soil and some flower seeds. I work from the tin boat, a slow process that requires repositioning for each hammered nail.

By the end of the day, all is ready for the sun and the spring showers. Margy comes back into the cabin, covered with dirt from head to toe. We're both tired, but both gardens, our floating stumps, and several decktop planters are ready. Now we wait.

As if on cue, a flock of birds arrive during March's first official week of spring. But they aren't swallows. Margy uses one of our bird guidebooks to identify them as Oregon Juncos, a breed of birds we have not seen here previously. They flitter around the birdhouses but refuse to enter. According to our wildlife books, the preferred nesting areas of these "snowbirds" are bushes and small trees. But these Juncos find an immediate food source – our newly planted floating garden.

At first, two birds swoop down and land in the garden. They could be after the grubs or nematodes, or they might be swiping our seeds. In any case, they are disturbing the soil and moving the seeds around as they peck and dig. I stand at the patio door, watching helplessly as they attack our floating garden.

"Maybe we should install the bird nets," I say.

It's an obvious solution. The nets are rolled up along the sides of the garden, ready to pull across the raised beds. Although not covered yet, we had planned to use the nets to shield the garden before our departure to the States in a few weeks, so the seeds would be protected as they sprout.

Before Margy can respond. I add: "I've changed my mind. Erase the word 'maybe' – let's get going right now!"

As Margy steps beside me at the door, we watch as two birds are suddenly joined by at least a dozen other Juncos – it's an outright air raid. Some buzz down in a quick touch-and-go; others land on the garden and walk around, contentedly pecking at the soil. As birds leave, others arrive, each time more and more, until at least twenty Juncos are simultaneously assaulting the floating garden.

Within a few minutes, I am on the garden float, which is still moored to the transition float. As soon as I arrive on the scene, all of the Juncos depart in a flurry of cheery chatter – *tsip, tsip, tsip.*

Margy assists me in unrolling the bird nets from the sides of the garden, using plastic clothespins to secure them to the six-inch-high side fences. I slide the tall daffodils, now in nearly full bloom from last year's bulbs, through the mesh. It's a tight fit, but most of these plants should survive fine. While we are attaching the netting with the clothespins, several Juncos return to invade the garden right where we work. The birds swoop close to our heads, land on the soil near us, and peck at the dirt right in front of us. Others somehow sneak through or under the mesh near the edges of the garden. I reopen a section of the net and shoo them out. They leave reluctantly. A few minutes later the netting is in place, securing both of the garden's beds.

Back on the cabin deck, I survey our work. Plastic clothespins now surround all sides of the garden. The fine-mesh net forms an opaque gray cover over the newly planted soil.

A Junco drops down onto the net. He lights for a moment and then begins hopping along the mesh. He bounces up and down, and then attempts to break through the net. The first Junco is immediately joined by another, and yet a third. They bounce up and down, looking for entry.

"They're using our net for a trampoline!" I yell to Margy.

It does look like that – Juncos bounce up and down on the netting as if it's some sort of game.

"There's one inside," says Margy.

"No way – cant' be."

"He must have found a way in. Oh, look there's another!"

Sure enough, two birds are somehow under the net, walking around and pecking at the soil. Several more birds swoop down and join the action on the trampoline. Now both nets hold bouncing Juncos, and within moments more birds have slipped through or under the netting.

"What's going on?" I exclaim. "They can't be getting inside. Our nets are secure."

"Secure, maybe. But I see at least four birds inside. Look, here come some more."

Juncos are everywhere on the garden float now, bouncing on the trampoline, and somehow sneaking through the netting.

When I arrive back at the garden, waving my arms and shouting ("Shoo! Shoo!"), the birds quickly fly away. Most of the birds below the nets exit with ease. How they get out so quickly is as mysterious as how they got in. One bird, however, is trapped in the netting and needs help. When I approach him, he panics and struggles. One of his wings is caught in the mesh, and it will be damaged if I don't act quickly. This is a beautiful bird, its black head and breast perfectly accenting a brown back and an underside that's pinkish-white.

I pull off the clothespins on the Junco's end of the net and tap on the side of the fence near the bird's wing, careful not to touch it. The Junco flutters loose on its own, then immediately flies out of sight.

When I examine the nets more closely, they seem to be firmly in place with the clothespins. How are these persistent birds getting in? While I scan the net where it meets the side fences, a Junco lands on the edge of the garden float, walks to the fence, and pushes inside. The fence holes are only a half-inch in diameter, but this bird has momentarily made itself small enough to squeeze through the opening. Our bird nets don't enclose the side fences, so the answer to the intrusion of the Juncos is obvious. We'll need to cover the sides too. But we don't have enough netting.

By now, stores that stock bird netting are closed, so we'll take the boat to town early in the morning. Besides more netting, we'll need a lot more clothespins and plastic edging to close the small gap at the

bottom of the fences. If these birds can scrunch through the small holes in the fence, they can also squeeze under the fence. This is war.

* * * * *

The next morning, we motor down the lake to the Shinglemill, and our truck is soon parked outside Canadian Tire, waiting for the store to open. We buy the last two available bird nets, two large packs of clothespins, and 25 metres of plastic garden edging.

We waste no time getting back to the cabin. The Juncos have already begun their morning activities, jumping up and down on their trampolines and casually stepping through the small openings in the side fences. A few Juncos are already under the nets, pecking at the soil.

It takes almost an hour to fully secure the garden. We add netting that extends below the side fences, place the plastic edging over the bottom, and add more clothespins than necessary. When we are done, we return to the cabin deck to await the next wave of invasion. It never comes.

Later that morning, a Junco arrives on the trampoline, jumps around for a few minutes, and then hops over to the edge of the float to check out the side fences. He pecks at the side netting for a moment, and then flies away. Another Junco arrives immediately, hops up and down on the top net for a few seconds, and flitters away. Except for an occasional Junco visitor over the next few days, the flock of black-headed invaders is gone. Maybe this was merely an overnight stop on their migration northward. But when free food in the garden was available, they turned a night's stay into a vacation retreat.

The swallows finally return in early April, and the beleaguered garden turns out its normal, healthy crop of vegetables. It's not clear who really won the war, but life soon gets back to normal at Hole in the Wall.

* * * * *

After the swallows arrive, two of the birdhouses on the shed get a lot of activity. The birds enter and leave, carrying trailing bits of twigs and grass that stick out of the door openings. One of the birdhouses becomes an active nesting site. Babies are soon chirping for food: "Feed me! Feed me!"

Margy and I anxiously await the sight of the new baby birds, which are still out of sight within the birdhouse. Mom and dad make repeated flights to and from the babies, bringing food. They swoop out over the floating garden, then low and fast towards Cabin Number 2 across the bay. Then back they come, taking turns diving down to the shed. After resting on the perch of the birdhouse for a few seconds, mom or dad hops inside, and then is gone again to repeat the whole process. The cry of a hungry baby bird (by now we think there is only one) goes on all day long, usually with a brief rest in late afternoon, then begins again near sunset: "Feed me! Feed me!"

After two more weeks, a little beak and a scraggly head peeks out through the birdhouse's small entry hole. Binoculars prove it is indeed a baby bird, a scrawny-looking and demanding youngster.

The baby's exit from the birdhouse should be soon, and the shed's location necessitates that its first flight will be over water. I wonder how many first flights are successful. Then again, this is coastal Canada, so birds here probably have a floatplane licence.

We wait. One day, the baby is crying for food, but mom and dad don't respond. Are they forcing their baby to vacate the nest?

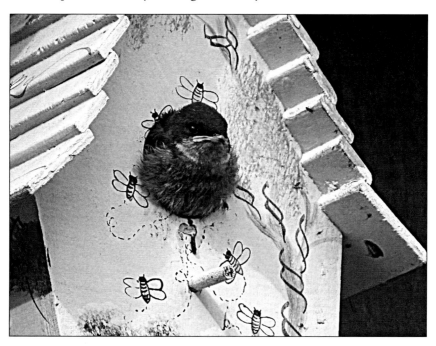

The next day, on a drizzly morning, we awake to silence. The normal morning cries for food have ceased. I walk out onto the cabin's deck and stare at the birdhouse with the binoculars, looking for any sign of activity, or any sound. Then a pair of swallows swing down over the floating garden, bank sharply to the left, and fly between me and the cabin, right under the porch roof and out the other side. One bird is full-size and expert in making its arcing turns. The other smaller bird is darting more than flying.

The two swallows arc back around the cabin again, as if to say "Thanks!" Once more, they fly under the porch and out the other end.

"Goodbye!" I yell. "Fly high and fast."

The two swallows zoom upward towards the cliff and are gone.

Chapter 8

Wood, Dogs, and other Staples

"Here come the Germans!" yells Margy from her floating garden. I'm standing on the porch roof, painting the upper portion of the cabin. This is a precarious position to be on any house, say nothing of one that floats on a lake. The Germans always enter and leave the Hole in the Wall at full throttle. On the way in, I sometimes wonder whether their powerful boat will be able to stop before reaching the back of the Hole. (We don't really call them "The Germans" – their true identity is disguised to protect the guilty. In case this reference to nationality offends you, please note that I'm of German descent.)

"They must not see me!" I yell down to Margy.

Not seeing a man on a roof at this close distance, with a bright metallic ladder extending up from the deck, seems unlikely. But they do see something else.

"Look, geese!" shouts the little girl in the boat, easily heard over the roar of the engine.

"Man on roof!" I yell, but loud enough to be heard only by Margy.

The Germans speed by Cabin Number 3, the wake of their boat rocking the breakwater and continuing onward towards the cabin. Margy bobs up and down on her garden, and water washes over her float logs. I hold onto the chimney and watch the paint splash in my bucket.

Repeated on-plane passes by the Germans is better laughed at than cursed. I go back to my painting, and Margy keeps picking strawberries.

* * * * *

When my new weather station arrives, it takes a full morning to assemble the components. My new equipment supplements a variety of weather instruments I already use, and fills a few gaps in my atmospheric measurements. As a weather junkie, I now have five digital temperature readings: two for outside locations, one for the living room, another for the upstairs loft, and even one inside the refrigerator (to monitor its temperature and the status of the propane supply). Two rain gauges and three barometers (a bit of overkill) are now included at my Hole in the Wall weather station.

Assembly instructions for the new anemometer (wind indicator) are particularly difficult to understand, but finally it is ready to mount. The intended location for the rotating cups and the directional vane is the tall wind generator pole that is high enough to provide a clear zone to measure the wind velocity.

I really should wait for John's assistance. I have neither the proper hardware nor the knowledge required for the correct mounting of the cup-and-vane assembly. But the anemometer is the most interesting component in the new package, so I refuse to wait. I rationaize that John can usually fix any messes I make, so it's safe to mount the equipment myself.

During the winter, winds on the BC coast approach hurricane velocity, which is precisely why I've looked forward to being able to monitor wind speed. I don't want to lose my new anemometer in a storm because of a shoddy mounting, but I do want to get it set up quickly. So I decide to make a temporary installation using what tools I have, until John is able to attend to the details.

I lean a ladder against the wind generator's pole, climb as high as I feel comfortable, and strap the anemometer to the pipe. The bolts provided in the kit are not long enough for this pole, so I use plastic ties to connect the device as tightly as possible. Just to be sure the wind doesn't whip away my new instrument in the next few days (although no storms are forecast), I use an excess of safety wire to secure the mounting plate. The anemometer might not make it through the night, but it won't be lost overboard into the water.

As I descend the ladder, I look back up at the pole with pride. It may not be John-tough, but it will provide me with wind data right away. The cups are already rotating on their precision bearings.

As I step onto the deck, Margy appears from around the corner. She walks over and stands next to me, as we both inspect the new addition to the pole.

"Oh, John's not going to like that," she says, shaking her head with concern.

It's not a criticism. It's an obvious fact.

* * * * *

"**Y**esterday's Toronto Stock Exchange was hotter than a parking lot in Port Alberni," says the early morning announcer on CBC radio.

He's referring to the record high temperature on Vancouver Island yesterday, a nearly unbearable 38 degrees C at Port Alberni. At the cabin, I recorded 37 degrees in the late afternoon, the highest so far in the midst of this mid-July heat wave. Today's forecast is for cooler temperatures, but with higher humidity and the possibility of thunderstorms. A Campbell River woman calls CBC's morning radio show to report thunder and lightning over the Strait of Georgia during the night: "Extremely wild," she says. "It's the first thunderstorm I've seen in three years."

Looking out my bedroom window in the loft, the sky seems clear, but all this talk is enough to get me out of bed and downstairs to check my weather instruments and survey the outside conditions.

From the deck, I observe a few clouds in the distant south; otherwise, the sky is completely clear. The morning temperature registers a comfortable 20, with 80 percent relative humidity. I could have left my telescope on the outside deck last night, but I decided to bring it inside under the threat of showers that never developed. The scope has been a fixture on the deck for three strait days and nights, tracking a large sunspot group during the day and deep sky objects on each moonless night. As much as I love nighttime observing, it was a relief last night to finally get eight hours of sleep.

The heat of the past few days has been a great excuse to do nothing – unless you consider the joy of reading and watching boats go by as

work. I'm never bored on my float and can't imagine ever catching
cabin fever here. But someday I may be proved wrong.

Today, my excuses to avoid chores are gone – the temperature
should be reasonable, and the woodpile needs tending. It's never too
early to stock up on wood for the winter, and already I'm behind
schedule. There are four steps to my on-going firewood plan. First
there's the gathering process, an easy procedure this year. Powell Lake
is at a record high water level, and that has drawn an unending wood
supply away from the shores. The past few weeks, the lake has been
full of floating debris, and much of it has drifted to Cabin Number
3. Each morning the firewood appears right off my deck, ready to be
hauled aboard.

Some of the wood is properly sized and ready to store for the winter,
but most needs to be cut (the second stage of the process) to fit into
the stove. Some of that wood has to be split (the third stage). The final
phase of my firewood gathering process involves moving the wood to
store it for the winter. Most of it ends up on the firewood float, in the
storage shed, or out under a flat-topped frame on the transition float,
between the cabin's main float and the bridge to shore.

The transition float will get my attention today. Much of the
wood that comes to us is hauled out of the water there. This float is
now heavy with clutter, which tends to sink its cedar foundation low
into the water. Because of the present high water level, the bridge to
shore now slopes downward toward the shore, in contrast to its typical
30-degree (or more) upward tilt. The lake's level is already four inches
above the previous high-water mark recorded during my seven years of
living on the lake – a yellow line with *6-2003* painted on the rock cliff.
The wide variance in water level each year (typically about 4 metres)
causes the cabin to rise and fall regularly, necessitating an occasional
adjustment to the cliff anchor cables and the chain that attaches to
the stiff leg. The lake's level is dependent upon the melting of snow,
precipitation, and the paper mill's control of the gates in the dam (as
determined by their need for electricity). Right now, all three gates are
wide open, and still the lake level is rising.

The cabin itself rides through this cycle unscathed. The biggest effect
of high levels of water is the jumble of wood that floats everywhere. The
flotsam tends to congregate in patches that are usually not seen until

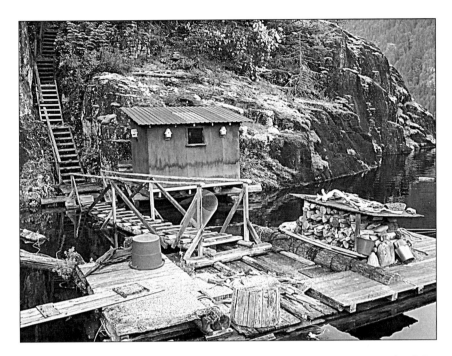

your boat is nearly on top of it. Recently, a boater going up the lake hit a deadhead (submerged log) that ripped the stern drive leg from his boat. Both the leg and the prop disappeared down to the bottom of the lake, an expensive accident. Regardless of these navigational hazards, we rely upon floating wood to feed our woodstove all winter long.

The woodpile task for today is easier than splitting logs, a job that I'll need to attend to soon. For now, I only plan to cut the smaller pieces of wood that have already been piled up on the float. It should be a simple job to cut the pieces into stove-size chunks.

Besides cutting and splitting, there's also chopping. Fortunately, chopping is not necessary for my firewood needs. It is the most labour intensive job of all, although seldom done by locals or even loggers these days. Originally, chopping was how you would cut down a tree, before saws came into use, but it is now nearly a lost art. Few old-timers miss it.

Even though today is T-shirt and shorts weather, I put on protective layers of clothing while using the chainsaw, which sometimes spits out splinters of wood. Just as I'm lacing up my steel-toed boots (also appropriate when using a chainsaw), I hear a loud *Boom!* It's a distant, deep, reverberating sound that passes right through the cabin walls. Margy and I look at each other – it's a sound we cannot identify.

Again: *Boom! Boom!* The cabin resonates in the wake of each blast.

"Dynamite?" I suggest.

I've heard road building before, and that blasting didn't sound like this.

"Maybe a landslide," replies Margy.

That's not it either. We've heard landslides before, a prolonged rumbling. Today's noise is best equated to the sound of giant machinery being dragged across the ground, vibrating across the lake.

"Look at the clouds," I say. "They're moving in fast."

In just a few minutes, the sky has gone from nearly clear to solid black with several bright blue breaks between the towering cumulus. The sound we've heard is thunder, but unlike any thunder I've ever heard before.

Boom! Boom! Then a lightning bolt strikes far off in the distance, followed by two more resonating booms, this time sounding like traditional thunder. As the storm drifts closer to us, the mountains and the lake operate in concert to focus the sound up the channel – a supernatural reverberating rumble.

"No chainsaw for a few minutes," I say.

My boots and suspendered coveralls are already on. But using a metal saw might not be the best idea in a thunderstorm.

The storm passes quickly, dropping a few large drops of rain while bold sunlight still shines. The lightning strikes become pronounced, more closely interspaced with thunder that rumbles along the fjord-like walls of Powell Lake.

With the short-lived storm now past, I finish dressing for the job of cutting up firewood. My outfit includes a hat with drooping ear covers, gloves, and big-cup ear defenders. Most of my body will be protected from flying wood chips. I decide to forgo my normal goggles for a pair of wrap-around sunglasses. Goggles create perspiration even on a cool day.

I carry the chainsaw and a sawhorse over to the transition float. The sawhorse is a hefty structure that John built for me after I destroyed a smaller model with a few errant strokes of my saw. This taller structure is perfectly sized for the task – simple but efficient.

I lift the first piece of wood onto the sawhorse, start the chainsaw (which uncharacteristically catches on the first pull of the cord), and begin to cut. Chunk after chunk drops off the end of the sawhorse, nice stove-sized pieces. Sweat builds up quickly under my shirt and coveralls, and soon I am thoroughly soaked. Perspiration runs down the inside of my sunglasses, and I have to stop periodically to wipe sweat out of my eyes. But, as is always the case when cutting wood, it's a thoroughly satisfying activity.

You've heard people speak of "going out to chop wood" as a stress reliever. This is not "chopping," but is similarly rewarding. My energy expenditure (and internal heat production) is significant, but the result is somehow deeply gratifying.

In a half hour, the chainsaw runs out of gas and quits. It's a welcome relief to take a break from cutting wood. A well-deserved swig of lemonade tastes wonderful!

I fill up the chainsaw with gas, add bar oil to the top of the reservoir, and resume cutting. When I'm finally finished with the firewood on

the transition float, I tackle a smaller pile that sits on the main float. Margy and I split our duties on a project like this. I do the cutting, and she does the sorting. Together we tackle the cleanup, including sweeping up the sawdust and hauling cut wood to the firewood float.

Margy gets the final job of sharpening the saw in preparation for its next use, having been trained by John for this task that I've never been able to master. After a day's cutting, she'll patiently hover over the saw at the picnic table with the file and depth gauge, bringing the old blades back to life by smoothing them at a precise 30-degree angle.

By the end of the morning, we have nearly a full month's supply of winter wood stored away. It's a never-ending process, a regular chore at the float cabin. But we enjoy the work. And, when we're finished, it's almost impossible to describe how wonderful it feels to strip down and jump off the deck into the cool water of our natural swimming pool.

* * * * *

In John's truck, we ride towards Lund on Highway 101. Bro is spread out in the front seat, catching a nap in anticipation of another busy day on the trail. That leaves little room for me, plastered up against the passenger door.

As the road winds through a logging slash near Gibsons Beach, a bear steps out onto the highway about a half kilometre ahead of us. The full-grown bear stops momentarily, and turns towards us, pausing right in the middle of the road.

"There's a bear!" says John.

It's a simple statement, only loud enough to attract my attention. But Bro immediately jumps up on the seat, fully roused out of his nap. He excitedly scans the horizon, and immediately goes into siren mode – a high-pitched shriek that Bro reserves for bears. The bear bounds off to the side of the road, quickly disappearing into the bush.

Surely, Bro has not smelled a bear from inside the truck, not at this distance. But he understands English, although probably only a few words. "Bear" is one word that always catches his attention. Bro knows bears.

* * * * *

At the airport, John and I try to repair an oil leak on the engine of the Piper Arrow. This is not a major leak, but every time the nose landing gear extends, the tire is spotted with oil. Today we have the engine cowl removed, and we're trying to find the source of the leak.

While we inspect the engine, Bro chases airplanes. It's innocent enough, since he never makes it all the way to the runway. When a plane lands, he rushes out of the hangar, barks his fool head off, and then runs back.

A light rain has been falling all morning, so Bro's occasional excursions towards the runway seem even more senseless. Every time he barks and runs off, John yells at him futilely: "Bro!" But the dog just keeps going.

I lie on the ground in the hangar, shining a flashlight up through the wheel well, while John tries to identify the source of the leak. He slides his finger under the oil filter and beneath several hoses that wind through the engine compartment. Meanwhile, a helicopter raises a ruckus outside the other end of the hangar – *whomp-whomp-whomp* – sounding like it's only a few metres away. And Bro is gone again, barking his head off.

"What the hell is going on?" yells John, over the racket created by the helicopter. "Where's Bro?"

The helicopter's *whomp-whomp-whomp* continues for a few more minutes, and then I realize it has been hovering nearby for quite a while. Now it's rotor changes pitch, as it lands and shuts down, just out of sight beyond the hangar. The rotor blade spools down, and Bro comes running back into the hangar.

"Where have you been?" asks John.

Bro barks twice in answer to John's question. A few seconds later, a man in a tan flight suit walks into the hangar.

"Hey, could you hold onto your dog?" asks the man. "I've been trying to land on the helicopter pad for the last five minutes, but your dog keeps chasing me. So I had to set down out in the grass."

The pilot is amazingly cordial, but a turbine helicopter quickly guzzles up expensive fuel. I look the other way, as if I know neither John nor Bro.

"Sorry," says John.

The pilot walks back to his helicopter, to move it back where it belongs. Bro barks again when the helicopter starts up and air-taxis

back to the landing pad, while John firmly holds onto him. When the noise stops, John lets go of Bro, and we go back to troubleshooting the oil leak.

* * * * *

Halloween at Hole in the Wall, with nobody home but me. No trick-or-treaters, and not even a ghost (I know they're out there). I go to bed early but am awakened by the sound of heavy rain, which might even be hail. It beats hard on the metal roof only a few feet above my head. In a few minutes the rain (or hail) stops. I lie in bed without going back to sleep. I'm content just to absorb the night. Stars suddenly appear through the bedroom window, proclaiming the passage of the cold front. I grab my flashlight and climb down from the loft.

When I step out onto the outside deck, the last-quarter moon is rising over Goat Island, so it must be about 3 am. Low scattered clouds are streaming northward through First Narrows. I scan overhead to find Cassiopeia, using the pointer stars in the "W" to lead me to Perseus. This is my first chance to view Comet Holmes, a normally faint comet discovered decades ago that is now in the news because of a sudden flare-up to third magnitude.

Just to the left of Alpha Perseus is a star that is not supposed to be there, and it's fuzzy.

I drag the plastic lounge chair out from under the porch and lay it out nearly flat. I lie down and train my binoculars on the nebulous patch. A bright comet leaps out at me. It has no visible tail (pointing away from earth), but boasts a bright nucleus – one of the most spectacular I've ever seen. I lie there enjoying the motionless show, until the cold of the first day of November drives me back inside.

By now I'm wide awake, so I decide to cook breakfast. When I'm alone like this, I enjoy a schedule that follows a disjointed sequence, which includes breakfast in the middle of the night. I cook up a big meal – bacon, scrambled eggs, and toast with peanut butter and blackberry jam, plus a tall glass of milk. By the time I go back to bed, it's nearly dawn.

I sleep contentedly, awakening again at 9 o'clock. Then I pack a knapsack, including a lunch of two roast beef sandwiches, chocolate chip cookies, and two cans of pop (one for John). I'm supposed to meet John at Cabin Number 1 to work on a project, and the day is turning out to be sunny and relatively calm. So I decide to take the tin boat on a trip considerably longer than the norm for this small vessel.

Before departing the Hole, I climb aboard the boat, taking a few minutes to try to solve an electrical problem involving the navigation lights that I have been troubleshooting for the past few days. I work from the aft seat, using my multimeter to check the circuit wiring that winds along the boat's port side. I use my foot to push the cruise-a-day gas tank out of the way to the other side of the boat. A few minutes later, while concentrating on the wiring (oblivious to everything else around me), I notice that my feet are cold. And soaked! The tin boat is filling with water!

When I look down, water is pouring into the stern, and rising rapidly! When I pushed the tank to the side, it struck the rubber drain plug at the bottom of the transom and popped it out of its hole.

I reach down into the water, frantically searching for the drain plug. The water is ice cold, and so is my hand. My feet are wet, my fingers throbbing from the cold water, and the tin boat is sinking right at the dock!

I consider abandoning ship, but surely I can find the plug or something else to stuff in the hole. There it is! – My cold fingers feel the rubber plug, and I ram it back in, twisting it tight.

I take a few moments to allow myself to calm down, and then I start bailing out the boat. When I'm finished, I go back into the cabin to change out of my soaked boots and socks.

Finally I'm ready to leave, but before I leave Hole in the Wall, I stop across the bay, where Jess and his father are constructing an enlarged cabin, using the original float cabin as one end of the new structure. In only a week, they have progressed to the point where the entire structure is framed, and much of it has already been covered by plywood. Jess's skookum new engine-driven barge sits out front, the perfect vehicle for hauling construction supplies up the lake.

I turn off the outboard motor and float outside Jess's breakwater, while he and I yell back and forth for a few minutes. I offer words of praise for the new cabin: "You're bringing up the property values in our neighborhood."

"My old cabin was just too small," says Jess. "You know: eight-by-ten, just like a picture."

The old cabin was one of the smallest on the lake, with barely enough room to sleep inside. By comparison, this new cabin will be a palace.

Leaving the Hole, it's a beautiful ride south, with morning shadows still casting long profiles on the east shore. The North Sea is almost flat, and the conditions on the lower lake are perfect for a small tin boat.

When I pull into the breakwater at Number 1, John is nailing two boards to the outer logs of the new float foundation that he has started to build – someday it will be Cabin Number 5. As if he knew I was bringing the tin boat today, he's preparing a dock properly sized for it. He pounds in the last nail just as I drift in against the boards.

We spend the day working on a ramp for pulling firewood out of the water. We haul two long logs up the steep bank, orienting them parallel to each other, to serve as the framework for the ramp. Working from a raft, John uses a long-shaft electric drill, powered by a gas-driven generator, to prepare the poles for metal rollers.

It's a warm first day of November, a fine day for work like this. Like all of John's projects, he maintains a constant eye for quality, what others might consider overkill. But to John, it simply has to be done right. And it's a great opportunity for me to learn some of his construction techniques.

After our lunch break, Rick arrives in his tin boat, a heftier design than mine, with the driver's seat at a forward console and a 35-horsepower Johnson for plenty of power. The four of us (don't forget Bro!) tackle what remains of the ramp project, making quick work of the final details.

By the end of the day, my muscles have received a noticeable workout. I'm glad to be able to help John as partial repayment for the multitude of tasks he does for me.

"I think I'll go now," I say, as the sun drops towards the Bunsters. "Unless you need me for anything else."

"You just want to go bombin' around in your tin boat," says John.

He's right. The trip back up the lake to Hole in the Wall is a fitting ending to a rewarding day – a closeup view of a comet, breakfast in the middle of the night, some work with a friend, and lots of bombin' around in my tin boat.

I glide close to Cassiar Island and out into the calm North Sea. Then I swing past Sandy Beach, with long shadows stretching out again – this time from the west. I aim my tin boat towards First Narrows, past the green navigation beacon that blinks in the twilight, and home to Hole in the Wall.

◊ ◊ ◊ ◊ ◊ ◊

110

CENTER-OF-BOOK ILLUSTRATIONS

Shinglemill Marina, Powell River BC

Gemini and Wayne at Hole in the Wall

Fritz and Shorty with Margy at Hole in the Wall

Paper Mill and Hulks Breakwater, Powell River BC

Willingdon Beach and Paper Mill, Powell River BC

Bob's Crew Boat at Hole in the Wall

Looking north over Powell Lake from Heather Main

Looking north towards First Narrows, with Goat Island at right

Chapter 9

Down the Lake

Amid-July trip down the lake is needed to take care of some chores in town. The bookmobile stored at the airport must be prepared for an upcoming sales event. While I'm at the airport, I can also take care of some minor maintenance on the Piper Arrow. In addition, a trip to town will allow me to check my email and pick up a few groceries – multitasking at its best.

This week, Margy's 91-year-young mother and our cat are on the float with us, so Margy and I are a bit nervous about getting stranded in town during this period of unsettled weather. July has not been as sunny as normal. Another storm is forecast to move in tonight, so I'll make the trip down the lake by myself. If I get stranded in town, Margy will be on the float to spend the night with her mom.

Things in town can take longer than expected, so I plan to give myself plenty of time. I'll leave at mid-morning, and my chores should consume only part of the day. I should be able to make it back to the Hole well before sunset.

I motor away from the breakwater in the Campion before 11 o'clock. Before even coming up on-plane, I make a quick stop at the cabin at the outer edge of the Hole. On the float's outside deck stands five-year-old Dominick, dressed in shorts, fishing hat, red life vest, and a big smile. As I pull into the breakwater, the little boy waves his fish pole in my direction.

"Be careful or you might catch a big one," I yell to Dominick as I approach. "And it might be the prop of my boat."

In defiance to my words, the boy retrieves his line and tosses his baited hook towards me. As I drift closer, engine now at idle, a small red bobber plops into the water well short of my boat. The Campion comes to rest next to the bobber, 10 metres from the deck.

"Could you ask your dad to come outside?" I ask.

Before Dominick can respond, Max steps out on the deck.

"He's gonna catch a big one," I say to Max, motioning towards my prop.

"If your line gets caught in that man's prop, do you know what happens to your hook?" Max asks his son.

Dominick continues to cast and retrieve his line, his hook and bobber falling just short of the Campion. On one cast, the red bobber whacks harmlessly against the stern, and settles a few feet away.

"Do you still need a refrigerator battery?" I ask Max. "I'm headed to town."

Yesterday, Max and Dominick visited my cabin in their tin boat, looking for a small 9-volt battery for the safety cut-off mechanism in their propane refrigerator. Without a battery, the fridge refused to function.

"Thanks, but Justin dropped one off for us. The refrigerator is working fine again."

Max's wife, Monica, joins Max and Dominick on the deck. We talk for a few minutes while I float near the cabin, with my engine still idling.

"Watch out with your fishing line," Monica reminds her son. "You're awfully close to that boat."

Dominick grins at Monica, but doesn't speak. Mischief in his eyes. He continues casting and retrieving his hook, seeming not to have heard any of our warnings.

Max and Monica haven't been at their cabin much this summer, but now they are making up for lost time. Max explains that it has been a battle to get the cabin back in shape after damage to their float during the severe winter. For me, it has been an easy task, mainly because I've been at my cabin almost continuously. Cabin maintenance is demanding, but you hardly notice it when it's spread out over the whole year. Of course, having John to assist me with the big tasks makes it lots easier.

While we discuss the challenges of cabin maintenance, Monica suddenly interrupts us: "Margy is trying to get your attention," she says.

I look back over my shoulder, and there is Margy on the deck of our cabin. From this distance, I can't see much more than a tiny figure standing on the deck, waving in our direction.

"Okay, see you later," I say to Max and Monica. "Anything I can get you in town?"

"No, we're all set," says Monica.

I shift into gear and pull slowly away from the cabin. Then I hear Monica yell to me: "I think he caught your prop!"

Looking back, I see Dominick pulling on his line, trying to free it, while Max says: "No, you need to let your line go loose, or it will break!"

I shift into neutral, but it's too late. I watch the boy's fishing line go taut. Dominick gives it a tug, and it breaks.

"I'll raise the leg and see if I can get his hook and sinker," I yell back to the cabin.

"Don't worry about it," says Monica. "We've got lots of hooks."

The little boy looks straight at me with a huge pout. The message is clear: this was his favourite hook and bobber.

"I should check my prop anyway, just in case," I reply.

I turn the engine off and use the electric trim to raise the leg out of the water. Then I step back onto the swim-grid and give the prop a cursory inspection.

"Nothing on the prop," I say. "See, I told you that you were gonna catch a big one."

Dominick directs another pout straight at me.

"Sorry," I say. "Mom and Dad will fix you up with another hook."

I lower the leg back down, restart my engine, and head back to find out what Margy wants. She is waiting for me on the deck, holding up a set of keys.

"I just wanted to make sure you have the keys to the car," she says.

Normally, we use the truck for our trips to the marina, but this time we have her mom's car. If I had gotten all the way down to the Shinglemill before discovering I'd forgotten the keys, I wouldn't have been pleased.

"I have my keys, but they're in the bottom of my pack. So why don't I take those, since you have them out."

I give the Campion a shot of throttle to drift closer to the deck. Margy and I have learned an important lesson for float cabin residents: never toss anything of value while on the deck of your floating residence. When the boat is nearly touching the deck, Margy carefully hands me her keys.

"Since you're here, why don't you check out that little stump," she says, pointing to a small floating piece of driftwood just outside the breakwater. "I can't tell from here, but it might be worth looking at."

We're always looking for prospective natural designs for the cabin. Small twisted pieces of driftwood make great deck ornaments.

After clearing the breakwater, I stop at the piece of floating wood, consider it appropriate for our deck, and haul it aboard.

Finally, I'm off (again), down the lake to town. Considering the delays in getting started, I wouldn't be surprised if today's trip takes even longer than expected.

* * * * *

On my way down the lake, I normally cruise past John's two cabins on the lower lake. Friends keep an eye on things for each other, and today I notice a problem at Cabin Number 1. The blue tarp over his old boat looks tattered. It now covers only the rear of the boat, and that will allow rainwater to build up in the hull. Considering the leaks already plaguing this derelict hulk, the approaching storm could be the boat's last gasp.

Cell phone coverage is usually adequate at Cabin Number 1, so I call John. He answers on the second ring.

"I'm floating off Number One," I announce. "The tarp on your old boat is almost completely off."

"I noticed that the last time I came down the lake from Number Two," says John. "But it was getting late, so I didn't have time to stop. The tarp is pretty well shot."

"Maybe it has just slipped off," I reply. "I haven't gone inside your breakwater yet, but I'd be glad to take a closer look."

"Sure," says John. "But don't work at it too long. It will be okay, even with the storm. It just keeps filling up, and I keep bailing it out."

After I hang up, I ease the Campion into the breakwater and tie up at John's cabin. Then I walk the shaky gangplank to the floating dock where the old boat is tied. The tarp has come loose, but it seems mostly intact, so I stretch it back over the boat and tie it as tight as I can. One of the tarp's snaps has broken, allowing the entire cover to slide off the boat. Large wooden blocks, tied to the edge of the tarp as weights, have been tossed to the boat's other side. It would have taken quite a wind to blow those blocks completely across the top of the boat.

Using a piece of safety wire, it takes only a few minutes to create a new connection to replace the broken snap. I connect the wire to a rope and then to an old nail that I pound into a nonessential spot on the old boat's front deck. I snug the tarp tight, ready for the incoming storm. In only a few minutes, I'm back in my boat and on my way again.

I finally arrive at the Shinglemill, nearly two hours after first leaving my float cabin – not exactly record speed.

*   *   *   *   *

At the grocery store, I find all of the items on my list and quickly make my way through the checkout aisle. At least something is on schedule. Since I'll need to dress in old clothes for the bookmobile painting project up at the airport, I take care of my store visits first, including a stop at Canadian Tire. Figuring that I am now operating on a more efficient schedule, I drive to the condo, take a hot shower, and climb into my old clothes. (I know that sounds backwards, but when you live in a float cabin without running water, you take advantage of a hot shower at every opportunity.)

I repack the few groceries that require refrigeration, placing freezer packs from the refrigerator into a small ice chest. Next, I'll be going to the airport, where the bookmobile is parked. From there, I'll return to the Shinglemill. My refrigerated items should easily survive the afternoon.

Now it's time to check my email and transmit the messages I've prepared in advance while back at the float cabin. Nothing slows things down more than a computer. Time to spare? – Try connecting to the Internet.

As the computer starts up, I glance out the window. The Texada Island ferry struggles against increasing ocean swells coming in from the southeast. Dark clouds are rolling in rapidly, casting a winter-like look over the harbour. I walk to the patio door and slide it open. Wind whips around the balcony, and the sound of sailboat tackle rattling in the marina below catches my attention. It looks, sounds, and feels more like January than July.

When wind whips up the Malaspina Strait like this, weather conditions can get worse quickly. In fact, they already have. The good news is that such storms tend to work their way into Powell River first, and then up the lake. If I react fast enough, I may be able to outrun the storm. But with any further delay, I could get caught in severe weather conditions going back up the lake.

As soon as the computer finishes starting up, I abruptly shut it off, without even checking my email. I'm out of here!

I get going fast. First, I drive the car down to the harbour parking lot where Margy's truck sits. I pull an empty plastic tub out of the car, unlock the rear of the truck's shell canopy, and swing the door upward. The wind catches the door and forces its closed again, right on my head. I struggle with the door and the small plastic tub, trying to transfer lime from a bag in the truck into the container. In the gusting wind, it's a futile task. Lime swirls all around within the truck's bed, and all over me. One of my tasks for this trip to town was to bring back lime for the outhouse. But in these conditions, it's not the worth the effort. So, with the plastic container still nearly empty, I slam the canopy door shut, lock it, and return to the car.

There's another job still undone, and it's the primary reason I came to town. But the trip to the airport to work on the bookmobile is now out of the question. Overhead, the clouds are now even blacker, roiling and spurting out big drops of rain.

I've carried books with me to resupply a retailer that is on my route back to the Shinglemill, so I decide to take the time to drop off the books. But when I try to pull up in front of the store, all of the best parking spots are already taken. I pull forward to a spot that will require a 50-metre walk in the rain. And by now, it's quite a downpour.

I wrap six books as best I can in thin plastic and struggle the short distance to the store. Wind whips around me. The brief weather window for a trip back up the lake may have already disappeared.

My business in the shop is quickly finished, and I'm back in the car in just a few minutes, and on my way again. When I arrive at the Shinglemill, the rain has eased up a bit. It's not that the storm has lessened. Quite the opposite – the storm is still developing, but it has not yet reached the Shinglemill. A few kilometres can make a big difference when a southeaster like this begins to roll in.

There's not much to load in the boat, so I need to make only one trip from the car in the rain. As I exit the marina, three boats are headed in, probably returning from their cabins before the storm hits. Most boats on the lake are headed south, while one is going north. It's a common situation for me.

The lower lake is already a bit rough, but within safe limits. White-caps are here-and-there, but conditions should improve as I travel north. Unless the conditions worsen, I'll be able to proceed at a comfortable speed of 20 klicks. Storms seldom move north faster than that. I should be able to outrun this one.

The conditions remain fairly stable, and the waves are well below my personal limits in the Campion. As usual, I follow the eastern shore, which provides considerable protection from a southeast wind. Once past John's Cabin Number 1, the lake's surface smooths out a bit. Passing the Washout (flooded nearly a century ago by overflow from Inland Lake), the waves are mostly gone.

The North Sea is barely rippled. This area can be nasty in a strong southeast wind, but I'm fortunate to have out-raced the storm. It's a

pleasant crossing to First Narrows and the protected area behind Goat Island.

I turn into Hole in the Wall, slowing to a no-wake speed as I pass Max and Monica's cabin, and maneuver between flotsam that is caught in the still waters. Here the rain is barely pitter-pattering down, and the water is glassy smooth.

In six hours I should have accomplished a lot more in town. But I bought some groceries and have returned safely. I'm glad to be home well before the storm hits in full fury.

* * * * *

It rains throughout the night. The next morning I'm jostled awake by blustery winds that take the cabin for a ride. *Whump!* – the cables reach their outward limit, and the cabin comes to a gentle stop, slowed by John's modified rubber tire shock absorbers. I go downstairs and check the barometer – it's rising rapidly.

The sun is above Goat Island now, and puffy cumulus clouds are mixed with patches of blue sky. By mid-morning, rain showers return, alternating with brief moments of sunshine.

After breakfast, Max and Dominick pull into our breakwater in their tin boat. I meet them outside, just as Max cuts the motor and drifts a few metres from the cabin's deck.

"Dominick wants to tell you about something he did," says Max.

The little boy looks sheepishly away, staring downward into the boat.

"I bet I know what happened," I say, trying to get Dominick to talk to me. "Did you catch a fish?"

That brings Dominick's attention up and out of the boat. He beams at me with excitement: "I caught a fish and ate it for breakfast!"

"Tell him how you caught it," prompts Max.

"I caught it with a bobber and a hook. No fishing pole," says Dominick.

"Oh," I wait for more, but that's all Dominick is willing to offer.

"After you left yesterday, we saw his bobber floating off our deck," says Max. "It was the line you cut, bobbing up and down with a fish on the hook. Had to chase it with our boat."

"What kind of fish was it?" I direct my question at Dominick.

"A rainbow trout," replies Dominick determinedly. "A big one."

He holds out his small hands, palms facing inward, about six inches apart. I look straight at him and smile.

"You see," I say. "I told you that you were going to catch a big one."

Chapter 10

Mowat Bay

*M*r. *Kayak* moves from salt to fresh water regularly. Although a sea kayak by design, this ultra-stable two-person vessel is a joy to paddle on a lake. *Mr. Kayak* has spent a good portion of its life at Hole in the Wall, and has completed voyages across the entire length of both Lois and Haslam Lake. With the kayak, we've camped overnight at Khartoum Lake and are always looking for variety in our journeys. So a visit to Mowat Bay was unique only in the sense that we had never paddled through the lower reaches of Powell Lake. As is often the case, the greatest adventures can be found close to home.

During a prospective warm day in late spring, an afternoon of paddling in local waters seems like a logical plan. *Mr. Kayak* is ready to launch, perched on the top of my Ford Tempo in the condo garage. In the spring, we are anxious to get back into the kayak, so a mid-June jaunt should be ideal for both paddlers and kayak.

Usually, in my haste to travel up the lake to my cabin, I avoid lingering in the lower portion of Powell Lake. Mowat Bay is a major launch site for local boaters, but it is a spot I seldom visit. Today, I take the right turn at Cranberry's main intersection and begin looking for signs for the road to Mowat.

"Is this the turn?" I ask Margy, as we approach a likely downward sloping street that juts off to the left.

"No signs," she replies.

But this looks like an obvious route down to the bay, so I make the turn. The street winds downhill, soon ending at the bay. Just past an open yellow gate, lower Lake Powell spreads before us.

"I guess you're just supposed to know how to get here without any signs," I state.

"If you don't know how to find it, you shouldn't be here," says Margy.

It's a common occurrence. I'm often enticed by advertisements I see in the local newspaper that include everything but an address. If you're a local, you're supposed to know where things are. If you're not a local, tough!

As we drive through the parking lot on the way to the boat launch ramp, we pass only one car. To the side of the paved area is a dirt parking lot with about a dozen trucks, all with empty boat trailers.

I stop next to the dual launch ramp that straddles a long dock that juts out into the water. There's no one on the dock, and the ramps stand empty. The weather has turned ugly, and the sunny breaks have disappeared, as a threat of showers blows in.

A dirt turnaround next to the dock is occupied by only one truck with an empty trailer, so I select this spot as a good place to park and wait for the imminent rain shower to pass. But I don't notice the steep lip leading into the dirt area, and the car bottoms out with a resounding crunch. This area is obviously designed for trucks, not wimpy compact cars. I struggle to turn around so we can overlook the bay. I avoid the major potholes, and pull to a stop.

Dark clouds stretch to the north and east. Conditions have changed from warm and sunny to brief spurts of showers. Spring is struggling into summer, as rain clouds come and go and the temperature jumps around.

As we sit in the car, huge drops begin to pound the windshield. It's intense for a few minutes, almost hail. Then, just before the rain stops, the sun pops out.

"Just a sun-shower," I say. "Neither sugar nor salt."

"What?"

"Didn't your mom use that one on you? I thought all mothers picked on kids who whine when it rains. We're neither sugar nor salt, so what's the big deal about a few drops of rain."

I move the car, careful this time, driving slowly back over the abrupt lip and out onto the pavement. I park on the launch ramp. It's an ideal place to put a kayak into the water, with a dock nearby to tie-up to. Usually, we launch on beaches that require a long drag out to the water, and where there's a big rush to move the car. Today we aren't in anyone's way, so we take our time getting *Mr. Kayak* into the water.

The sky is clearing now, but the towering dark gray clouds to the north still look threatening. The wind is gusty, but there are no significant waves in this sheltered bay. As we organize our equipment on the dock, a family of geese swims by, all in a line. The young geese are getting big, but are still easily distinguished from their larger parents – mom leads, then the youngsters, then dad.

When we cast off from the dock, I get the fun of steering with the rudder pedals. I aim for the east shore, where two boys are jumping off the cliff into the lake below. They probably swam out to this spot, since the overland hiking route is quite rugged. Although Powell Lake's water is still mighty cold in spring, the boys act like it's mid-summer. They hurl themselves off the cliff in cannonball style, splash around briefly, climb back up the rock wall, and plunge back in again.

We follow the shore northward, passing alongside the towering cliffs. Soon we round the bend to the wider portion of the bay. Boom logs are meticulously chained together here, all parallel to the shore.

"Good looking logs," I note.

As residents of the lake, we're into logs. Areas where they float and accumulate are always of interest to lake people.

"Must be an old float cabin site," replies Margy. "But I don't remember ever seeing a cabin here."

"These logs are too good to be abandoned. They must be used as pens for the logs they bring down from the Head, or maybe they use them to move stuff around in the bay."

Mowat Bay is a major log booming site. It's the destination for all of Powell Lake's towed booms and the launch and recovery spot for logging equipment. We've never ventured close to this shore with our boat, so the sight of these high-quality logs is new to us. (Later, John explains that this booming area has been used for decades, most of its logs being destined for regional sawmills.) I'm amazed I've missed this area of the lake, so close to our home at Hole in the Wall. As is often the case, the biggest discoveries are near your own back door.

Booms of logs, chained end-to-end, continue around each indentation of the bay. Just when I assume it will end, another crevice in the bay leads to more logs. Every once in a while, a strategically placed boomstick protrudes perpendicularly from shore, keeping the line of logs about 5 metres away from the shore. The continuous line extends well over a kilometre, finally ending at two rafts carrying winch equipment and a small storage shed.

Under still-threatening but dry skies, we paddle farther north to Haywire Bay. The lake here is nearly calm, and paddling is easy. We weave through Haywire, past the picnic area on the beach, and around a small island where three tents are pitched, one with a large blue tarp

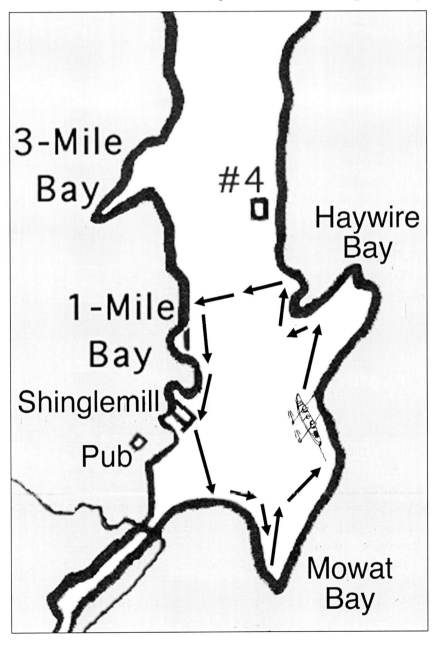

to extend its territory. We paddle behind the peninsula, into a small bay where swimming is popular, but the water is too cold today. A submerged stump sports a sign that warns: *No Lifeguard.*

We pause near the peninsula, bobbing on the dissipating wakes of boats that pass well offshore. Then we start across the main body of the lake to the opposite shore. Since the wind is a bit stronger and more northerly here, I push the kayak's rudder pedals to aim slightly north. This heading should cause our track to arc nearly straight across to the other side of the lake.

"Guess what we forgot?" asks Margy.

We always forget something when kayaking. It's a tradition.

"I give up. What?"

"Our flag."

We usually mount a small Canadian flag atop a tall pole on the stern, to increase our visibility to other boat traffic. It's a bad thing to forget, so maybe we're fortunate to be in a lake that might be considered the flotsam capital of the world. Boaters here are always on the lookout for debris that can damage their props and hulls.

"We're bigger and brighter than most logs," I note.

The kayak is yellow and we wear bright life vests (Margy's is yellow, mine is red), which should help identify us to passing boaters.

As if on cue, two boats appear on the otherwise empty lower lake, one headed south and one north. They will meet nearly at mid-channel, and that is precisely where we are headed.

"Speed bump." Margy reminds me of what boaters sometimes call kayaks.

"And that ain't all," I reply. "There's a floatplane that looks like it's ready to land."

Sure enough, as the boats converge towards us, a seaplane drops down over 3-Mile Bay, headed east, and then turns south to land along the shore near John's Number 4 cabin, a few kiometres north of our current location. We watch the plane land, taxi a short distance, and then apply power again for takeoff directly towards us.

"Touch-and-go," I state. "Or do you call it splash-and-dash for floatplanes?"

"Wouldn't want one of those to land on top of us," quips Margy.

"I'm sure floatplane pilots are even more attentive when it comes to logs and other debris than are boaters. It wouldn't take a very big log – or kayak – to ruin your day on takeoff or landing."

The two boats pass well in front of us, while the seaplane climbs out overhead. It's a lot of activity for such a small part of Powell Lake on a late afternoon in spring.

As we cross the open water, the sun comes out from behind a line of gray clouds. The sun's heat, coupled with the energy we've exerted by paddling, causes us to sweat. So we stop to remove our jackets. Pulling off a jacket (under a life vest) is not an easy process in the tight seat of a kayak. The first elbow is the hardest. But we both finally get our jackets off and stow them behind our seats.

Reaching the west shore, I use the rudder pedals to angle *Mr. Kayak* along the steep rock wall that leads all the way south to the Shinglemill. The wind from behind us adds a nice push.

We stop paddling for a rest. The kayak continues to move along at about 2 knots, pushed by the wind. Red-barked arbutus trees, only a few metres away, seem to grow right out of the rock. Yellow flowers in full bloom are interspersed with the arbutus, speckling the surface of the cliffs.

Besides having a tailwind, there's the lake's usual drift. It too is pulling us to the south. I call it the "tide," but it's the result of water being drawn towards the paper mill's dam. The repositioning of the gates causes regular changes in the rate of flow. Today we can simply sit and watch the scenery go by, taking advantage of the combined wind and current.

At the Shinglemill Marina, we pass close to three float cabins that are now docked at the north end of the breakwater. Each of these cabins is undergoing major renovation. Two months ago, the smallest of these cabins looked hopelessly deteriorated. Now it is covered with new siding, and has been extended to nearly twice its original size. The deck of this float cabin has been substantially reduced in the process, but the overall improvement in appearance is amazing. All three cabins seem well on-schedule for return to their mooring sites by the beginning of summer, which doesn't truly arrive until July on the wet west coast of British Columbia.

We swing around the marina's boom logs and tie up at the end of the dock reserved for visiting boats. Two more families of geese swim between us and Glen's wooden tug, which is docked at an adjacent finger.

Inside the pub, we order the Stanley Cup Special, a pound of chicken wings for $5. Margy looks at me inquisitively as the waitress asks if we want anything to drink. We are safety-conscious about not drinking alcohol when driving, boating, or flying. Where does paddling a kayak fit in? We each order a pale ale with our dinner.

"Could be a PWI," I say. "Paddling while intoxicated."

"Easy does it," replies Margy.

The television in the pub is tuned to the hockey finals, and I watch the customers as they keep a keen eye on the game while eating their meals. One family of six has moved their seats to make sure their view is unobstructed. As we order our meals, there is a tremendous round of cheers.

"Sounds like Edmonton scored," I say to the waitress.

She shrugs. I get the feeling she wishes she wasn't working here on a hockey day with a noisy crowd.

After dinner, it's an easy launch from the dock. We haven't even bothered to remove our neoprene kayak boots for our visit to the pub, so we're ready to go. We push off and paddle strong and steady. The meal and brief rest have invigorated us rather than leaving us sluggish. Maybe the beer helped.

The water is considerably rougher now. As soon as we leave the marina, we encounter two-foot waves. While paddling parallel to the waves, we're pushed continually towards the south shore, so we angle back out to compensate. These swells are not nearly as large as we've had to paddle through on the chuck, and they are spaced close together. This gives the waves less time to produce a rolling motion. The water merely slaps at us, occasionally splashing over the sides into our cockpits. Only a small amount of water gets aboard, and *Mr. Kayak* remains comfortably stable. But it takes a lot of paddling to make good forward progress.

We pass another float cabin under construction near Block Bay (named after the shingle blocks towed to this spot). This cabin is being built from scratch. We've watched its construction over the past six months, and it's now approaching completion. Although the cabin is new, it doesn't have a new site on the lake. There's currently a provincial moratorium on additional sites, so this float cabin will replace an existing cabin somewhere on the lake.

The toughest part of this segment of the trip comes as we try to round the point where Block Bay transitions into Mowat Bay. A log boom extends out beyond the promontory, requiring us to paddle directly into the waves. Finally, we round a 2-metre-diameter floating drum that marks the end of the protruding boom, and we slip into still water on the other side. From here it is an easy ride with the wind at our backs.

We ease up against the empty dock and haul ourselves out of the kayak, a process that is never graceful. Margy and I sit on the edge of the dock, feeling exhausted.

We watch the sun paint the remaining clouds with a brilliant red as it drops below the hills to the west. A kayak trip, even a short one like this, leaves you with a good feeling of accomplishment, and with a reminder that it's one of the best forms of exercise – for both mind and body.

Chapter 11

Boat Ride

"Can I help you work on your bridge today?" I ask John over the phone.

His bridge to shore at Cabin Number 1 will require lots of grunt work to replace the main supports, and John has made it a priority. This morning, I sit on the deck of my float cabin, talking to John in town. We often plan out our days this way.

"Thanks, but I've got a bad back. Must be something I did when trimming the hedges at Elizabeth's house."

John has been battling back pain for the past few days, but it hasn't slowed him down.

"Maybe you should crawl under your truck. That should help."

"Hey, I tried that yesterday! It didn't work."

"I know. I tried to call you last night, but Rick said you were under your truck."

John has been under his truck a lot lately, trying to track down an oil leak.

"Maybe we could go for a boat ride," he says. "That would be good for my back."

It's good for backs; great for almost any ailment. It's still early in the day, so we could go to the head of Powell Lake, if we can figure out how to manage our gas. My Campion would be best for the trip, but the fuel gauge sits well below the half-tank mark. I suggest we use a five-gallon can that I have in reserve here at the cabin, and John can bring an additional container of gas from town. That will provide plenty of fuel to get to the Head and back, with enough extra to make it down the lake to the Shinglemill tomorrow.

"I need to fix that switch anyway," adds John, as if we need an excuse for the trip. "I can do that first. Then we'll go for a boat ride."

The master switch that controls the solar panels at my cabin is broken, and I'm temporarily limited to using only one panel for power. During the long sunlit hours of summer, that's not a problem, but it's nice to have plenty of electricity for cabin lights during the evening. With the switch repaired, I will be able to run on one set of batteries during the day, leaving the others for nighttime lighting. John can fix anything.

"Okay, come on up as soon as you can, repair the switch, and then we'll get going."

* * * * *

John flips the switch behind the cabin back and forth, while I stand inside the den, yelling at him through the wall.

"It's on," I report, as the bulb lights up.

"How about now?" he asks.

"Nothing – Oh, just kidding."

"Don't do that," snarls John. "I need to wire this up right."

"Otherwise the garage door will keep going up and down?"

"Or the TV goes off," he says.

Within a few minutes, the switch is rewired, and the entire solar system and batteries are back in business. We move a cruise-a-day tank from John's Hourston to the Campion and hop aboard. John hops into the driver's seat, assuming his usual position, while Margy rides shotgun. Bro jumps aboard at the stern and immediately rushes up to the bow. I unhook the lines and step into the front of the boat. Bro and I are now separated from the rest of the crew by the walk-through windshield.

The Campion's bowrider design is perfect for me. I'd just as soon ride as drive, stretched out in the open air of the bow. Of course, it's a seasonally dependent position, and this is the beginning of bow-riding season. In fact, today is the first day of the year that I can ride up front without being forced back under the canvas by cold air. I'll ride here even in marginal conditions, but today is expected to be unseasonably warm, with a forecast high of 24 degrees C. It's not quite summer yet, but it marks a good start toward the warm months and many glorious rides in the bow.

Leaving Hole in the Wall, John brings the Campion up on-plane, and I settle in with my back against the cushions below the windshield. Bro takes up his customary position at the point of the bow, poised

like an observant scout. But he's a scout who pants a lot while riding in boats. Every once in a while, the 50-klick airflow catches the dribble from his hanging tongue, and a bit of dog drool hits me in the face. But it's Bro, so it's okay.

Entering the open water between Olsen's Landing and Second Narrows, the water becomes amazingly calm. This is often a rough spot, but not today. The surface is without a ripple. The mountains to the north catch the morning sun and are reflected in the water in front of us.

After Beartooth Creek, snow-fed waterfalls dominate the mountain walls on both sides of the narrowing lake. Most are visible only where they make their final plunge, but a few larger falls are visible all the way up to the top of the precipitous slopes. Where the waterfalls tumble into Powell Lake, nutrients plunge through the water, creating great trout fishing holes. We stop to fish at the mouth of such a cascade, right where it emerges from a ravine in vertical plumes of white.

Two docks straddle this waterfall, marking access to separate logging areas and new stretches of road building. The first dock has a crew boat tied to a small float that can handle one boat on each side. The second landing, another half-kilometre up the lake, is more extensive. A yellow crew boat is parked there, with room left for several more.

At the waterfall between the docks, John turns off the engine and lets the Campion glide towards the churning water. He immediately

heads for the bow, his favourite spot for fishing. I squeeze past him on my way back to the stern, where I join Margy.

"We'll sneak up on 'em," he says, as the boat glides within ten metres of shore and is immediately pushed back by the strong current.

Bro stands up on the bow cushions, next to John, hoping for a snack of fish heads. John casts out his line a few seconds ahead of Margy and me, his spinning lure hitting the water right at that perfect spot where the plunging water swirls in a white froth. *Bam*! – he has a fish!

"First line in the water wins," he says. "Feels like a nice one."

I set down my pole and go forward to assist in landing the fish. It's a 12-inch trout, caught by John on a barbless hook within seconds of his first cast. I grab his line and raise the fish out of the water far enough to give John a close look and to get at the hook with my pliers.

"Looks like a rainbow," I say.

This lake is full of cutthroat trout, but this fish has a wide pink stripe along its full length and lacks the cutthroat's red slash under the jaw.

Once fully out of the water, I grab the trout and begin extracting the hook. But as the fish flops around on the line, it breaks itself loose from the lure and plops back into the water. Since we're catch-and-release people, this just makes things easier.

After the first catch, John restarts the motor and repositions the boat back near the falls. Again, we drift outward quickly. Both Margy and John have strikes, but the fish don't stay on their hooks long enough to reel them in. As for me – nothing.

After John moves the boat in towards the white water pool for one more round of casting (and no more fish), we move on. Often, if you catch a fish right away, it runs around telling its friends not to bite. At least it seems that way.

Leaving the falls, we ride north past the second dock where the yellow crew boat is parked. As we pass, we examine the area in anticipation of exploring it further on the way home, when the logging crews will likely be gone for the day.

* * * * *

When we arrive at the Head, John maneuvers the Campion towards the far north shore, where stumps stick out of the water. He slows the boat to a crawl and uses the electric trim switch to tilt the motor upward.

"Lots of snags here," says Johns. "Some are right below the water, impossible to see if you're moving too fast."

I stand in the bow to look for submerged wood as we plow slowly ahead. John stands too, sticking his head out of the unzipped canvas over the center of the windshield. He keeps his right hand on the wheel, driving while standing, carefully scouting for obstacles.

"It's a spot that's hard to see until you're on top of it," says John, referring to a place on the shore where he plans to dock against a log. He knows this lake well.

"There it is," he says, pointing to something that has meaning to him, but not to me.

We pull up against a log that has fallen into the water, protruding out far enough to form a perfect floating cradle for landing. It's deep enough here to prevent damage to the boat, but close enough to shore to allow us to use the log as a bridge. After tying the boat up to the fallen trunk, John gives Bro an ass-push to encourage him to hop out.

Once out of the boat, the dog has no problem trotting along the top of the log to the beach. We follow, but moving a lot slower across the log than Bro.

John leads us up a short path towards a small cabin that is hidden from boat traffic on the lake by the surrounding trees. This is the lower cabin that survey teams from the paper mill used in past decades to check on the Head's water level, when boats were slow and the trip up the lake from the mill was more than a day's voyage. Another survey cabin, a few kilometres up the ridge, was used to determine snow levels and the potential spring melt. The upper cabin (*Up the Main*, Chapter 18) is constructed of sturdy yellow cedar, and is a much more elaborate structure than this one. Both cabins still stand ready for anyone who needs a place to stay in an emergency.

We eat our lunch near the cabin, where a sign proclaims *MacMillan Bloedel*, one of the early pulp mill owners in a long line of company names. Then we explore up the nearby hill and back down along the beach. Within an hour, we're walking the log back to the boat.

After a few more fishing stops (with no luck), we end up back at the waterfall where John caught a trout on his first cast of the day. John sneaks in slowly, ready to cut the engine when we are in close.

This time, I'm ready in advance, already standing in the stern with fishing pole in hand. There's no way John will get his lure in the water first, since he has to move to the bow after he turns off the engine.

As soon as he stops the motor, I cast towards the edge of the white water pool. I remind John and Margy of my self-proclaimed fishing proverb.

"First in the water catches the only fish," I predict.

My lure hits just inside the white water, and a trout immediately hits my red-and-white daredevil.

"Got him!" I yell.

"Oh, no. You beat me," says John. "It's probably the last fish we'll catch here."

The ten-inch trout – this one is a cutthroat – has swallowed my hook, so I make a bloody mess on the side of the boat as I pry the hook out of its mouth. But this fish may survive okay, judging from his energetic flopping around in an attempt to get back into the water. The trout swims away eagerly when I release him. It's the last fish we catch in this spot, regardless of two more tries at positioning the boat near the base of the falls.

We slowly motor over to the smaller of the two logging docks we saw earlier. The work boat is now gone, so we have the place to ourselves.

After tying up, we climb the newly bull-dozed road that leads past an ancient-looking crane. A huge log "jib" protrudes out of the front as a boom extension. Such old logging equipment is often left in-place long after its original function is complete. Many pieces of equipment like this have been sitting around in the bush for decades. In this case, it's difficult to tell whether this is another discarded piece of history or a relic that is still in use.

We climb up farther along the road to an area John hiked to years ago with Rick, before this road even existed. He leads Margy and me to a small waterfall where he remembers soaking in a natural rock-enclosed swimming pool on a hot, summer day.

"Not as good as I remember it," says John. "It seems like the waterfalls have grown bigger, but the pool is clogged by fallen logs."

"It always seems that way when you go back to a place where you've had fond memories," says Margy. "It's like trying to capture something spectacular in a camera. When you see the photo, it's never quite the same as it was when you were there."

I like the spot, and I ask Margy to take a photo of John and me in front of the small falls. Bro, of course, horns his way into the picture.

When we get back to our boat, we decide to stop at the other dock, although we can see the work boat is still there. It's close to quitting time for the crew, considering their long ride back to Shinglemill, so

we can probably go for a hike without concerning them. But if the crew is still building a road, workers (especially supervisors) can get very upset if you are anywhere in the area. Dynamite blasts create flying rocks that are dangerous.

Road Cruise, an appropriately named road-building crew boat, is tied to the dock. Its oxidized grey welded aluminum hull is capped with a bright yellow crew cabin. We tie up on the opposite side.

A red-lettered sign greets us on the shore: *Caution – Road Building. Do Not Proceed without Permission.*

"Interesting sign," I say to John.

I sense that I'm about to fight a loosing battle with John. I've lost many times before.

"We're just going for a hike," replies John. "We'll stay away from them. You can hear their equipment way up there."

John points towards the north, to the right of the new logging road that winds upward in front of us. John can hear things that I'll never detect, and there's no doubt that he hears the road building equipment.

"We'll hear them better if they set off some dynamite," I joke, but I'm not in a humorous mood.

The danger of being blasted to smithereens is low on my list of concerns. What really worries me is a nasty confrontation with the road-building crew. They can be very territorial.

I've been down this path before, and it isn't a pretty picture. I remember a confrontation between John and a logging boss on Goat Island that made me hope our boat was still in one piece when we returned to the dock (*Up the Lake*, Chapter 8).

"Let's go," says John. "By the time we get back, they'll be gone."

"I hope our boat will be here when we return."

It's a subtle attempt at a reminder of the Goat Island incident, but John ignores me. In that instance, our boat wouldn't start when we returned to the dock, and I immediately suspected sabotage by the logging crew. We quickly determined the problem to be merely a loose fuel hose, but I still wondered how that hose came detached.

"What's this?" asks Margy, looking down at the hard-packed gravel near the sign.

"Blasting holes," replies John. "They're all set to dynamite this area. See, the holes go all the way up the road."

A line of 3-inch-diameter holes, with small upside-down plastic cones inserted in them, are scattered every few metres. Water fills the cones.

"What are the cones for?" asks Margy.

John stoops down and grabs a cone, pulling it out of its hole. Water splashes on the ground. (John, do you have to touch that?!)

"Just covers, to keep dirt out of the holes. See?"

"We see!" I say. "Careful, please. What's the water for?"

"Oh, just rainwater. The cones keep that out too. Don't worry, they won't be blasting this area today."

That's reassuring. How does he know this? Is this hike really worth it?

"Since they're quitting soon, why don't we just wait until they come back to their boat," I suggest. "Then we can ask permission to hike while they're gone. I bet they won't mind."

This is a futile attempt at a compromise, and I know it.

"The sign doesn't mean anything," says John. "It's there even when they're not blasting. Whose forest is this, anyway?"

I knew it. We're going hiking.

John rushes ahead, using the initial slope to stretch his muscles. Margy and I start upward reluctantly, already well behind during the first part of the hike.

"That went well," says Margy.

"About as well as expected."

We pass a spur where a water truck is parked. The rest of the wide open area is empty, but this is where the road-building equipment will soon be returning.

John waits for us at an intersection only a short distance above the dock. The main road goes right, to the north. Another spur cuts to the left and sharply upward.

"They're working over there. Do you hear their trucks?"

"I think I can hear equipment," I lie.

"We won't be anywhere near them?" he says.

"At least we'll know where they are when the rocks start flying," I say.

"No way! Not today."

Treads in the dirt made by heavy equipment lead to the right, so we turn left. As we climb higher, the slope steepens even more.

"How do logging trucks drive down these roads?" I ask. "Darn steep."

"Not easy," says John. "And if the brakes give out, it's all over. All they can do then is aim the truck towards the shoulder and jump out."

I'm starting to huff and puff now, but John seems unaffected by the steep climb. I fall behind a little, and Margy follows even farther behind me. John is gradually outpacing me, and I'm doing the same to Margy.

"I wonder where this road goes?" says John, yelling back to me.

Meaning – we will be going up and up until we are totally exhausted, probably all the way to the end of the road. I've been in situations like this before, and John won't want to stop. Fortunately, that should take us farther away from any dynamite blasting.

I glance back at Margy. She is pushing hard but having a difficult time. I too am at my limit, feeling the fire in my lungs. John disappears around the corner in front of me and yells back: "Darn!"

Could be good news.

As I round the corner, I see what John has seen – the end of the logging road. Dirt is piled in huge mounds, marking the current extent of road building on this spur.

"Bad news!" I yell back to Margy.

"End of the road?"

"That's it," I yell. "We'll have to turn back."

"Too bad," she replies.

So ends our climb. We don't hear any dynamite blasts, and all ends well. But I swear I won't give in to John ever again. Until the next time.

Chapter 12

StickTail on a Float

Let me introduce myself – my name is StickTail. I'm a typical alley cat, but my human thinks I'm a Norwegian Forest Cat, an expensive cat you'll find at fancy cat shows. When I showed up on Wayne's kitchen chair, curled up and ready to take up residence, I was greeted with a growl of "Get out!" On my third visit to the chair, I was finally accepted. If humans don't want cats to visit them, why would they have such an inviting kitty-flap entrance built into their back door?

Confusion about my background continues to this day. Wayne still calls me "Norwegian" at times, since he thinks I am an escapee from a cat show. It is true that such a show was in progress at the nearby Los Angeles Fairgrounds the week I arrived, but actually I was a wandering feline who simply found a way in. Just before my arrival, I spent several days in the wild, where I had a close encounter with a coyote. That mean ol' critter bit off the end of my tail, a major *Ouch!* Thus, my first ride in a car was to the vet for tail surgery. Ever since, I cry mournfully when I ride in cars, disliking drives in vehicles almost as much as I hate swimming.

The photo of a Norwegian Forest Cat that my human found in a magazine did look a lot like me. And it is true I have many Norwegian characteristics, including a love of forests and rain – so maybe I'm not your typical cat, after all.

After a decade of comfortable living in California, I became very attached to my human. Any pet knows how emotionally involved you can get. So when my human moved (more or less) to Canada, it became difficult to be away from him for such long periods of time. And, sadly, each absence grew longer.

During this trying period, I was well taken care of by David, an experienced house-sitter and cat-sitter combined. But still I dreamed of being with Wayne up in that floating cabin that he constantly brags about. I'm sure he wanted me with him in Canada, but it was impossible because of the frequent trips back and forth. As an indoor cat (necessitated by the dreaded coyote gangs in California), it was a wonderful dream to imagine myself roaming free at a floating cabin. From the photos I saw, it was obvious that I wouldn't be tempted to go beyond the cabin's float because of the water, that tall cliff, and steep stairs to shore. I don't mind rain, but don't forget – I hate swimming. I visualized myself climbing under the float structure, catching mice, watching Canadian geese, and maybe even snatching an occasional trout. A cat's dream come true!

When Margy's mom moved to Bellingham, it was a great excuse for me to move closer to Canada, with the possibility of an occasional visit to a float cabin. Besides, every 91-year-old lady needs a cat, or so I told myself.

* * * * *

My journey to Bellingham was by airliner, with a change of planes in Seattle. By the end of the day, this major event was just a terrible memory. Adding to the horror of the travel, on the last leg of the journey, I was mocked by a little girl who thought it was funny to imitate my mournful cries inside the noisy cabin of the jet airplane.

After a day that I'd rather forget, I finally settled into a quiet and comfortable condo in Bellingham. We sent David a photo to relieve his heartbreak at losing me.

Safely in the Pacific Northwest, I quickly adapted to a life of luxury and loving attention. One day though, I knew something was up. Suitcases were being packed, always a bad sign for those who hate to travel. I was abruptly uprooted, put into a car, driven to Powell River (surviving an international border crossing and two ferries), and placed in a noisy boat. A half hour later, I emerged from my carrying case, and found myself inside a floating cabin. It was a nightmare getting there, but finally my dream had come true. The next day, I was out on the float structure, exploring my new world. And what a world it turned out to be.

The travel routine back and forth to Canada became frequent, although I have never completely adapted to cars or boats. I still live in Bellingham, but I visit Powell Lake regularly. Lately, I've been thinking: "What better retirement spot for a Norwegian Forest Cat (or a reasonable look-alike) than a float cabin in British Columbia?"

* * * * *

From Wayne's point of view:

Gemini is a motorless, classic old boat that sits docked behind Cabin Number 3. The boat serves as my writer's retreat, complete with a futon, computer table, and enough solar power to keep my laptop running all day long. Since the *Gemini* refurbishment project wasn't completed until the end of summer, the writer's retreat didn't see much action until the following year. But during the winter, with the assistance of a propane heater, I was able to spend some quality writing time in *Gemini*.

One of my goals has been to take *Gemini* out into an open stretch of Powell Lake and just drift all day – writing and relaxing. It's a getaway retreat that can really get away. But without an engine, I'll

need to tow *Gemini* to its ready-to-drift location. Then, I'll raft the tin boat to the side and settle in for a relaxing day of drifting on the lake.

The first opportunity for such a journey arises when StickTail is at the float cabin, so I decide to include him in my adventure. Maybe he'll enjoy a lazy day aboard *Gemini* with his human. But the noisy tow to the starting point for the drifting voyage will not be his favourite part of the journey.

On the morning of the excursion, StickTail knows something is up. Cats are smart that way – somehow StickTail always knows when someone is going on a trip, and he doesn't like it. He sniffs around the tin boat, as if he knows this vessel has something to do with what is about to occur.

I use the mooring lines to move *Gemini* out from its docking space, located behind the cabin. I reposition my writer's retreat and its tin boat tug near the firewood float. From there, it will be a short tow out of the breakwater.

I load lunch and beverages (including kitty snacks, of course), three fishing poles, two partially read books, and my laptop computer. This will be more of a test cruise than a writing session. But maybe I'll

write a chapter about drifting around a lake in a motorless boat with a long-haired, black cat as the distinguished passenger.

Powell Lake, like other large lakes and inlets in this region, is subject to inflow winds during the heat of summer days. Chippewa Bay can be rough under such conditions, since it is positioned at the end of a long stretch of open water on the lower part of Powell Lake – not unsafely rough, but motion-sickness rough for cats from Norway. Although there are many places where I can drift for hours without hitting shore, Chippewa is worth a try because it is near to Hole in the Wall. Few boats go in or out of the large bay, allowing me to avoid the concerns of passing boaters who might feel compelled to investigate a drifting boat (as they should).

As I carry StickTail to *Gemini*, he remains amazingly calm. His little heart doesn't go *boom-boom*. Instead, it's more of a faint *pitter-patter*, as if he understands this is supposed to be a gentle ride in a quiet boat.

StickTail will ride in *Gemini's* cabin, while I use the tin boat to tow us to where we'll begin our drift. I'll start with a tow rope that is only a few metres long until we clear the breakwater. I've never towed

another vessel with the tin boat, but I have plenty of rope standing by, if needed.

It takes a bit of maneuvering to clear the breakwater. Once outside the wooden boom, I let out 30 feet of rope and try to settle into a

straight tow, but *Gemini* S-turns erratically behind me. A prolonged tow seems impossible with this length of rope, so I add another 20 feet, and the boat settles down nicely. By the time I enter First Narrows, I'm able to increase the throttle to about 5 knots, with the tow line remaining nice and straight. Still, it will be a long haul to Chippewa Bay at this speed.

Looking ahead towards the North Sea, conditions look good. But a light inflow breeze already ripples the water near Sandy Beach. Coming around the point that separates the Narrows from Chippewa, I catch a glimpse of whitecaps. The water ahead does not look any rougher than expected, but it is rougher than I had hoped for. The waves may settle down as I proceed, but often it's quite the opposite. Today is no exception.

To orient *Gemini* properly so that the waves will push us into the bay, I'll need to continue ahead several more kilometres. Then we'll be able to drift back into Chippewa. I watch the red boat behind me as it pounds into the waves, wondering how StickTail is doing.

* * * * *

From StickTail's point of view:

How am I doing? How should a cat like me be doing in such circumstances?

Answer – not so good. I'm crouched under the futon, the only place I can find to hide from the horror of this sea voyage. After finally arriving at the much-anticipated float cabin and spending a few glorious days exploring the outside world on and under the float, now I'm here – rolling back and forth in a boat while waves slap incessantly at the hull. My keen inner ear throbs in agony!

Wayne promised me that this would be a short ride. He even used the word "smooth." So far, it's been neither.

And where is the bonding between cat and human? Here I am under a couch, while Wayne is somewhere out front in a noisy tin boat, driving us headlong towards our destruction.

Here, under the futon, I feel the rocking back and forth, and I hear the waves slapping loudly only a few inches below me. This is definitely not a pleasure cruise. So far, it has been a pure nightmare. In my recent journeys, I've been car-sick and air-sick. Now, stand by for sea-sick. Oh, my aching tummy.

* * * * *

From Wayne's point of view:

Finally, we're in position to begin a long, leisurely drift. I turn off the outboard motor and use the tow line to pull myself back to *Gemini*, where I hear a distressed cat crying inside.

With all the rocking and rolling that's going on, it takes a few minutes to secure the tin boat against the fenders that dangle from *Gemini's* side. As I try to raft up, I bang against the boat a few times. At one point in the awkward process, waves push me behind *Gemini*, where I whack hard against the stern. Thank goodness there's no engine to hit and John isn't here to see such inept maneuvering.

When I finally climb aboard *Gemini*, StickTail is doing fine, although I can see that he is not entirely happy. He sits on the futon (rather than under it – a good sign), but looks like he'd rather be somewhere else: *Meow*!

I try to coax him out onto the broad aft deck, where there is lots of sun and the motion of the waves is less noticeable. But the black cat refuses to budge from the security of the cabin. I sit down next to StickTail on the futon, and he brushes up next to me, demanding attention – another good sign.

I rig up a fishing pole for trout. We are drifting at an ideal speed for trolling, although it seems a bit futile to fish in this deep water. Then again, I've good lots of time and a good distance to drift.

The waves push us into Chippewa Bay faster than I expected. We are headed towards the only area where there are float cabins, so it will be necessary to move the boat soon. Maybe this is as good a time as any to simply get out of here and try somewhere less rough.

The tow out of Chippewa is clumsy – safe but time consuming. At first, the waves are off the bow, which makes towing easy, although slow. Then, as I round the promontory, the waves pound against the starboard side, pushing both boats towards the rocky cliffs. I have no problem keeping us away from the shore, but the bow angle causes prolonged slaps from the waves. I look back at the big red boat, knowing StickTail is not enjoying this in the least.

Under conditions like these, taking the shortest route is best, but that route parallels too close to shore. With the waves pushing us relentlessly in that direction, I think about my small outboard motor, an engine not known for reliability. I hope it doesn't quit, because getting it restarted can sometimes be a prolonged process, and the cliffs are too close for comfort.

Finally, I round the point, with First Narrows visible ahead. Almost immediately, the waves lessen. There are no more whitecaps, and conditions look better ahead. I turn off the motor and watch *Gemini* begin to drift. Once the big red boat settles down, I'll raft up to its side again.

As I wait, *Gemini* starts toward the cliffs. It isn't a fast drift, but enough to get my attention. I have turned off the motor a little too soon, and now I'll need to get it restarted – fast!

I pull and pull on the starter rope, open the choke, try advancing the throttle, another squeeze of the fuel bulb, another pull. Hurry! *Vroom-vroom* – the engine finally starts, and I tow Gemini away from shore just in time. There's a lesson here – have the engine running whenever you are near shore, even if you don't think you'll need it.

Once I'm a reasonable distance from the shore, I cut the engine, and we settle into a nice drift towards Sandy Beach. In fact, although it's impossible to judge yet, it looks like we may clear the beach and drift right through First Narrows. I rig up a fishing pole with my trusty red-and-white dare-devil as the lure of choice for drift-trolling, and settle down with my laptop.

In just a few minutes, I hear a boat approaching, slowing as it comes near. I glance out the window to find John moving closer in his Hourston. It's a big lake, but John can always find me.

As John approaches, he shifts into idle and then drifts towards *Gemini*. I step out onto the aft deck to greet him.

"Hey, man! – Your ground rod is broken," yells John.

I lean over the transom and look down at the metal rod that connects the boat's electrical system to ground (water in this case). The rod dangles from a thick wire, its two mounting screws sheared. I thought I'd gotten away with something, but John has caught me, as usual.

"I had trouble rafting up in Chippewa," I reply. "Must have smashed into the ground rod with the tin boat."

"I knew I shouldn't have left you alone," says John.

He rafts up on the side opposite the tin boat, and we drift and talk for a few minutes.

"Better get ready to tow yourself out a bit farther," he says. "It looks like you might hit the beach. Lots of underwater stumps there, you know."

"I thought I might drift right through First Narrows. But it doesn't look so good now. I'll keep my eye on it."

"Be ready," he says. "Even if you don't need it, have the engine running."

It's good advice that I could have used an hour earlier.

John pushes away from *Gemini*, restarts his engine, and leaves for his cabin at Hole in the Wall. A few minutes later, I climb aboard the tin boat and get the motor started. By the time it is running smoothly, I need to get busy maneuvering us away from Sandy Beach. I stay rafted to Gemini and easily guide both of the boats away from the beach with a short spurt of power. I leave the engine running as we drift towards the green navigation light, then out into the Narrows.

When I'm sure we'll clear everything, I shut down the outboard motor. Waves are almost nonexistent here, and it looks like the light wind will eventually push us towards the next point, at least 3 kilometres ahead. On this trajectory, we might even clear the shore for many kilometres beyond.

In a few minutes, we drift past the entry to Hole in the Wall. Margy calls on the walkie-talkie to report she has me in sight and asks where I'm going: "North," is my reply.

"Don't forget you've got to tow *Gemini* all the way back," she says.

"Someday."

I stand ready to start the outboard, in case the next bend in the lake proves to be an obstacle. But it isn't. In fact, we drift nearly right down the middle of the channel, northbound in wind-rippled water – perfect conditions. Elvis Rock is next, but it looks like we'll clear that too.

I retrieve my dare-devil lure, just to be sure the hook is clean. On the way in, a good-sized fish strikes – *Bam! Bam!* Then it is gone.

The water is flat now, with barely a breeze from the south, but StickTail refuses to venture out onto the aft deck. I sit on the futon with him, drifting and tapping keys on my laptop computer, writing this chapter.

As the sun drops towards the mountains in the west, I close my laptop and read for a while. Then I stretch out in a chair on the aft deck, catching some rays. Every half hour, I check the fishing pole – retrieve the line and then let it back out again – trolling while drifting along.

Boats are everywhere today, taking advantage of a perfect July afternoon. They run around me in circles – water ski boats, jet skis, boats pulling kids on tubes. Everybody gives me a wide berth, and I enjoy watching these sleek craft riding on their white pads of foaming water.

Gemini has passed her first test cruise in style. What better way to celebrate the majestic scenery and the fine weather of summer than drifting along in a motorless boat – with your cat, of course.

◊ ◊ ◊ ◊ ◊ ◊ ◊

Chapter 13

Circumnavigating Goat

During January, a change in plans regarding an overnight stay at the head of Powell Lake results in another circumnavigation of Goat Island, but this time during the winter. A planned overnighter at the Head is thwarted when the weather forecast abruptly changes. Strong southeast winds are now expected, so I phone John to discuss the situation.

"I'm worried about the winds," I admit. "The marine forecast calls for the next storm to move in tonight, although today still looks pretty good."

"You don't want to be at the Head during a storm," John quickly agrees. "But it's nice here in town this morning."

"Here too. Feel like going for a boat ride instead? Maybe up to Olsen's Landing or over to the new logging area near Henderson Bay?"

John is usually ready for a boat ride, but I don't expect such an immediate response.

"I'm on my way," he replies.

He hangs up on me before I can say goodbye.

* * * * *

An hour later, John charges into the Hole in his Hourston. His quick response to our change of plans deserves a reward, and Margy and I have it waiting for him. We've packed our personal gear and lunch, and are standing on the deck in our winter gear, boots, and life vests. Usually John needs to wait around (impatiently) for us to get packed up. Today we greet him, all set to step aboard the Bayliner.

My preparation of the Bayliner is another pleasant surprise for John. I have removed the cover from the command bridge, the engine compartment battery switch is turned on, and the key is in the ignition. John loves this boat as much as Margy and I do, but a trip on Powell Lake is usually made in the Campion, in the Hourston, or by using our tin boat. By comparison, the Bayliner is a gas guzzler. It's at our cabin for winter storage, but I often use the big boat for routine trips on the lake, justifying its use as a way to keep the engine in good operating order. Today we'll use it for a luxury cruise, with little more purpose than a bit of exploring. We owe it to ourselves.

"I see the top's off the Bayliner," John smiles as he steps out of the Hourston.

"We were gonna' take it to the Head anyway," I reply. "Can't disappoint a trusty boat, you know."

John nods his head approvingly.

On his trip up the lake this morning, John noticed a large dark object moving in the water, mid-lake just south of Three-Mile Bay. At first he thought it was a bear or an elk swimming across the lake, which would be a rather unique sight. But when John approached closer in his boat, he discovered an even more unusual spectacle – a black wolf about twice the size of Brody. The wolf began to spook, swimming erratically, so John pulled farther away and watched from a distance until it reached the western shore. The wolf clambered out of the water and shook itself off, now staring intently at John. No longer afraid, the proud animal then turned and sauntered off into the woods.

Imagine a wolf swimming several kilometres across a cold Canadian lake during January. What natural event or ingrained survival instinct would cause a pack animal to undertake such a crossing? None of us could come up with a good answer.

* * * * *

John and Margy climb upstairs to the command bridge, while Bro and I stay downstairs in the cabin. I'm recovering from a cold, so I'm glad to relinquish the open air bench seat. While traveling in this boat, there is no question regarding who will drive, so it's only a matter of who will sit with John as a passenger. It's the way we all prefer it.

John slips into the captain's seat, gives the throttle four shots of prime, and cranks the brand-new starter. The engine rotates smoothly.

The starter may be new, but it wasn't easy to install. Last week John lay awkwardly across the cold metal gas tank in the engine compartment, installing the new starter into its recess near the stern. It's the most remotely located engine accessory, and the hardest to reach. Today, the new starter performs flawlessly.

We cruise slowly north, checking out the cabins along the shore. A recent cluster of severe storms has taken its toll. Several cabins are floating at odd angles, still awaiting their owner's repair after the damaging winds.

I spend most of my time down below, out of the wind. Occasionally, Bro climbs down the steps into the cabin, but he stays for only a quick pat on the head and then returns to his watchdog perch on the aft deck. He prefers the open area, walking from side to side, checking out the scenery and trying to catch the scents of distant animals.

Every few minutes, I emerge from the cabin and climb part way up the stairs to the command bridge to converse with John and Margy. I watch over their shoulders as we motor northbound past Elvis Rock. But Elvis is still missing. His wooden image, holding a guitar, has

disappeared. We can't tell if poor Elvis is lying on the ground or has been swept out into the lake. In any case, during one of the recent storms, Elvis definitely left the premises.

Powell Lake Resort, on the west shore, is our first stop. John maneuvers the boat to the least deteriorated section of the old dock, and we climb the steps to shore. I lag behind, taking photos, while Margy and John explore the maze of trails that surround the cabins.

The resort is currently for sale, having been inactive for several years. A caretaker makes an occasional visit to look after the place. The asking price is $450,000, which includes an old diesel boat. But the land is a Crown lease, so it's difficult to imagine paying so much for the property. On the other hand, it's hard to understand how a resort, built in such a majestic location, would not be a booming success as a tourist destination. But getting here even in a fast boat is a 40-minute ride, or two hours in the resort's old and slow *Mugwump*. Tourism enterprises on the lake have never prospered, even with the gorgeous setting and easy marina access provided at the Shinglemill. Historic Rainbow Lodge, farther north, is currently for sale for nearly a million

dollars. Fiddlehead Farm, a commune-like resort to the south, was briefly successful, but was sold several years ago. Its buildings were left to decay, and the land was immediately stripped of its timber.

When I reach the cabins, there's no sign of John and Margy, so I explore a few of the trails on my own. I walk uphill on a path behind the cabins until it turns into more of a stream than a trail. The rain from recent storms has turned the paths in this region into temporary creeks. Another trail, with trees tagged for logging, leads downhill. I follow it for a while, but turn back after a few hundred metres. I return to the open area near the cabins, where I sit on the steps of one of small cottages taking in the beauty of the cloud-capped peaks on Goat Island.

I hear voices back by the dock, so I climb back down to meet John, Margy, and Bro. We share some candy bars and then push off.

John drives the Bayliner north along the shore, where we find a floating blue plastic barrel. It's a 45-gallon model, unlike the standard 55-gallon drums used for cabin flotation. It should be a good barrel for a small float, so we spend some time recovering it from a cove that is jammed with floating logs.

John treats the retrieval operation with care, maneuvering slowly so that our propeller isn't damaged for sake of an old barrel. I climb around the command bridge on the catwalk and go out onto the bow, where I will use a rope to lasso the blue drum. John carefully steers the Bayliner towards shore, keeping the prop in the deep water. I loop a rope around the end of a small log that is preventing us from getting close to the barrel. John backs the boat away while I pull the log away from shore. When John pulls forward again, I slip a rope around the barrel, and slide it along side the boat to the aft deck so we can haul it aboard. John comes down from the command bridge to assist Margy who is trying to raise the drum high enough to drain out some of the water. With the barrel's weight reduced, John hoists it into the boat.

Another kilometre to the north is Olsen's Landing, where we tie up to a old but sturdy float that is covered with brush and small trees that sprout from the its old water-soaked logs. This is one of the biggest docks on the entire lake, and it's been here for decades. From this location, loggers shuttle up Olsen Main and into Theodosia Valley.

Three pickups and a huge forklift are parked next to the dock, standing idle on weekends. Today is a Saturday, so we are the lone visitors to this normally busy dock. On a workday, this spot would be hopping with activity.

I walk up Olsen Main a short distance, to a place where the snow is fairly deep. Raccoon tracks cross the road, and I follow them for a while. Raccoons are plentiful in this area. Their cute little paw prints enter and leave the main for as far as I hike up the road. Finally, I stop at a spot where I can look down on Olsen Creek. It's running strong, but ends in a delta that is a mass of logs and foam-tossed flotsam. From up here, it's impossible to tell where the creek ends and the lake begins.

Back at the Bayliner, we pull out our camp chairs, and eat lunch. I bite into a meat loaf sandwich that tastes particularly wonderful in these surroundings. Why is it that food tastes so amazingly superb when surrounded by such majestic scenery?

Underway again, John motors slowly past a spot just north of Olsen's where several cabins once stood hugging the shore, tucked into a small flat plain hemmed in at the base of the mountains. Fast-growing alders have overtaken the area, but it is easy to imagine that this spot was a comfortable residence for the locally famous Olsen family. Remains of the old cabins sit just out of sight, hidden behind the trees that ring the shoreline.

John turns the Bayliner across the lake towards Second Narrows. When he advances the throttle, I step down the ladder from the command bridge and head back into the warmth of the cabin. I maneuver around Bro who is now looking a bit cramped, with the camp chairs and a 45-gallon barrel sharing the aft deck. I take pity on him and remove the folding chairs, stowing them back inside.

We breeze through Second Narrows, slip along the edge of the bay at Rainbow Lodge, and glide past an active log booming area just south of the main building. We continue down the east side of the lake, past a few floating cabins with smoke pouring out from their chimneys. Not many cabin owners spend winter nights on the lake like we do. Maybe these are day visitors who are firing up their wood-burning stoves and checking out their floats after the latest storm. Meanwhile, they can enjoy the relatively warm sunny breaks on a weekend in January. These few signs of activity are more than I expected for this arm of the lake, located over 20 kilometres northeast of the Shinglemill.

We pass a float cabin that was almost obliterated in a recent storm. It now rides precariously on its float, with its deck mostly ripped away. The roof of the porch droops low over the water, with both corner supports dangling in mid air.

Continuing south, the snow-covered mountains behind us poke through the clouds. Patches of blue stand out behind the high peaks. Multiple layers of stratus clouds flow down the steep slopes in broad sheets. An eerie sight.

We slow to examine an area where the winds blasted over a low saddle from Goat Lake. Along the shore, at least fifty trees were either blown down or their trunks were snapped off. Farther uphill, an open logging slash is now covered with fallen trees that have been tossed into the open area. The water area near two nearby float cabins is also covered with downed trees. Several of the trunks lie within a few metres of the cabins' roofs. The shore is littered with fallen timber,

their tree tops pointing out over the water, indicating the direction from which the crushing flow of wind came.

We cruise back towards First Narrows and Hole in the Wall, following the shoreline of Goat Island, and then across to the south side of the lake. At the logging dock near Fiddlehead Farm, two crew boats are tied up. Logging activity at Powell Lake has been more extensive on weekends lately than in previous years. The logging companies need to make up for lost time. A series of sixteen storms have plowed through the area already this winter. Even the normally weather-resistant logging enterprises had to stand down during these grueling times. Now the profusion of blow-downs have begun to rot, and loggers need to salvage as much of the timber that they can.

John spies another blue barrel. He slows, trying to decide whether to deviate off our course to pick it up. I know what he is thinking – he always has a difficult time passing up a blue barrel that could be used in the future for cabin flotation, but he also knows it's our gas. Margy notices his reaction and simply says: "Go get it." John is off in a flash.

This barrel is barely floating, with both of its caps missing. It's the standard 55-gallon drum, the larger variety. We sling a rope around it and drag it a short distance up the side of the boat. There's no way anyone could lift a filled barrel. But if you carefully position an open cap right at the waterline, the water will *glug-glug* out. Within a few minutes, the barrel is light enough to haul aboard. Brody now sits wedged against two blue barrels.

Our final stop is the new logging area near Henderson Bay. For the past few months, a private logging contractor has been building roads and dropping logs into the water at this spot. This is our first chance to explore the area.

A crew boat is at the dock, and another boat is tied to the boom where a dozer (boom boat) plows back and forth, reorganizing the logs. We pull into the dock and climb the bridge to shore. A narrow foot-trail leads to the staging area where heavy road-building equipment sits. John and I start up the main road, while Margy explores on her own and takes photos of the dozer's boom-building activity below.

John, Bro, and I walk up the road past fresh-cut cedar logs that are over a metre in diameter. This is prime timber, but not the kind of cedar John wants to buy for the new float cabin that he plans to build. Cedar has become valuable as lumber, so finding good logs to use as flotation is not easy these days.

"These logs are beautiful," he explains. "But it's second-growth, too green to use for a good float. The logs aren't cured like dead old-growth trees."

"So you couldn't use logs like this for a float?" I ask.

The logs are hefty and strong looking, fresh and healthy.

"Oh, you could use them, but they're not the best for a float. I need old-growth cedars, especially those that are fire-charred. But they're hard to find, especially logs like that in good condition."

So it's a situation that's difficult to solve. You need old logs, but most old logs are rotten. And no one wants to sell you good old logs, because they are valuable for lumber or to cut into shake blocks. So you're stuck until the right deal finally comes along. John is always looking for the right deal.

We walk farther up the hill, where the road gets muddy. Smaller trees that have been stripped of their bark are heaped along the sides of the road. These are mostly firs. We look down over the booming

area and out across the lake. From here we can see First Narrows to the north; just beyond is Hole in the Wall. We've almost completely circumnavigated Goat Island on this mostly cloudy but gorgeous January day.

We finally turn around, walk down the hill, and hike the trail back to our boat, where Margy is waiting for us. At the dock, the sun breaks out briefly from behind the clouds that hover above the broad Bunster Range to the west.

John and Margy climb back up to the command bridge, while I remain down below inside the cabin. Bro tucks in next to two blue barrels on the aft deck, and we head for home.

Chapter 14

Winter in the Hole

November is often the most exciting month of winter. Of course, November is technically autumn, but the weather is usually the most severe and winter-like of the entire year. It is the month when an abrupt change in weather conditions is expected to occur, and coastal British Columbia seldom lets us down.

Typically, November weather is stormy for days on end, with wound-up low pressure systems blasting out of the north Pacific, and right into the BC coast. Tightly packed isobars in these intense extra-tropical cyclones generate winds near and sometimes exceeding hurricane velocity. Since local residents are not yet punchy from months of endless rain, they are often awed and even inspired by the dramatic change of seasons. In contrast, by late December, the locals have become bored and saturated by the ceaseless onslaught of rain. By January, everyone is dreaming of an airline ticket to the sunny south.

* * * * *

On a mid-November evening, I sit in the second row of spectators at the City Council meeting. The mayor has invited me to address the council regarding my newest book, *Up the Winter Trail*. The community cable TV crew huddles over their equipment in the rear corner of the room near an open window. They need the window for a cable feed down to the first floor, so they leave it cracked, allowing the wind to make its way through the opening and into the meeting room in noisy bursts of cold air.

As the evening progresses, the wind gusts increase, and the window rattles with greater force. Everyone notices, including the mayor, who occasionally glances towards the corner. We all know a major storm is moving in tonight. If the forecast is to be believed, winds of 100 kilometres per hour are expected, with 70 millimetres of rain.

I make my presentation. The City Council seems to like it. The mayor holds high a copy of *Up the Winter Trail*, as if he is a commercial announcer. With the book still facing the TV camera (I hope they are zooming in), he says a few kind words. I reply by describing my book as "an attempt to capture the uniqueness of winter in our area." Then I add: "Maybe it's beginning tonight." There are a few chuckles. Everyone knows exactly what I'm talking about.

As I complete my presentation (with a scattering of applause from a small audience), I walk back to my seat. The councilman at the end of the table says: "I hope you're not traveling back to the Hole in the Wall tonight." That's a good sign – he's read one of my books.

"No, I'm in town for the night."

But I would have been out there on my float for this storm, if the council meeting hadn't been scheduled for this evening. The next day, I realize how fortunate my timing has been.

* * * * *

The following morning I stand at the condo's patio door, looking out on a raging chuck. The Comox ferry has not arrived, an indicator of the severity of the storm. The *Queen of Burnaby* is still in its berth on Vancouver Island. Amazingly, the Texada Island ferry is just pulling into the Westview dock. As vehicles carefully drive off, the vessel rocks and rolls against the pilings.

On a day like this, nearly all southcoast ferries will be cancelled. Yet, the Texada ferry still plies through the relatively protected waters between Powell River and Blubber Bay. This morning, "relatively protected" is a matter of perspective.

Two tugs towing large barges are in a holding pattern just offshore. They circle around in pounding waves, unable to proceed and unable to come to shore in these conditions. Tugs haul their cargo day and night, under the most demanding sea conditions. Today, through my binoculars, I watch as they orbit between Westview Harbour and Harwood Island, huge waves crashing over their bows, loads floundering behind them.

The rain comes down in sheets, driven nearly horizontal by blasts of wind. The windows in the condo rattle, and the trees near the harbour bend in the gusts, spring back, and then veer over again. By noon, peak winds of 105 kilometres per hour are recorded at the Powell River airport.

The entire town is in lockdown. You can move, but not far. The ferry that links us with the city of Vancouver is shut down, as is our connection to Vancouver Island. There are no newspapers, because there are no ferries. Even the local newspaper is affected, since it is printed on the Island.

The bus to Vancouver is cancelled, having no ferry to carry it south. It's amazing how much is affected by a disruption in ferry service. To make matters worse, Pacific Coastal has cancelled all flights. We are like an island, cut off from the lower mainland.

Walking to breakfast along Marine Avenue, there are spots where my forward progress is completely halted by the wind. It doesn't blow me over, but it does obstruct forward movement. Storms like this are ushered in by southeast winds. Malaspina Strait funnels the treacherous airflow between Texada Island and the mainland, magnifying the force.

The Strait of Georgia is a mess. Whitecaps begin right outside the marina's breakwater and continue as far as the eye can see. I estimate the swells near the harbour at 2 metres in height, even bigger farther out.

Nature has prepared this region for rain, and lots of it. The ground is covered with water-absorbing vegetation. Flooding is uncommon, but today's deluge is too much. Powell River is spared, but many nearby communities suffer from mudslides along streams that feed into lakes and reservoirs designated for drinking water. Radio announcers list the communities where water must be boiled. Electrical lines tumble, and BC Hydro is busy restoring power. Roads to remote areas are closed. We get off easy.

Fortunately, our local lakes can accommodate the excess water, since their winter levels are low from an unusually dry summer. Float cabins merely move higher alongside the shores where they are moored. Eventually, anchor cables must be adjusted, but it's not an immediate priority.

The pounding wind and rain continue throughout the morning, with the early afternoon looking a little brighter. Out over Vancouver Island, there are actually patches of blue. Tug traffic remains in offshore circling patterns all afternoon. It takes a long time for the chuck to settle down after a blow like this.

The forecast suggests further improvement towards evening, with a shift to strong northwesterly winds. Flow from the northwest indicates clearing conditions, and such winds are usually less severe. If there is any way to make it back to my cabin today, I'll go for it.

My plan is to hold off on the trip to the grocery store until the last moment. Then, Margy and I can load the boat, take a look at the lower end of the lake, and still cancel the trip, if necessary. A final decision is not needed until we are ready to leave the Shinglemill. Even then, we can turn back if the wind and waves don't cooperate.

It's November 15th, and the grocery store is packed. One lady complains that the crowds are big because the weather was so bad this morning. I think its because its payday at the paper mill. We stand in the checkout line behind three other customers with full buggies. We have our typical two-buggy load in preparation for whatever happens up the lake.

"Looks black outside," says the young female checkout clerk, when it's finally our turn. She motions over her shoulder to the wall of windows at the front of the store.

"Actually, there are blue patches over Vancouver Island," I reply.

Sometimes you say what helps you to rationalize what you want to believe.

"Still looks bad to me," replies the clerk.

We are in a race against weather and darkness. I'd like to wait a few more hours to assure the front has comfortably passed, but going up the lake at night is not for me. The trick is to wait as long as possible, without risking a trip in the dark.

At the Shinglemill, we load our groceries into the boat beneath foreboding skies, but the rain has stopped. Gusts still swirl in the marina, but I've seen a lot worse. The lower lake looks fairly calm.

Margy and I launch the Campion just before sunset, but already it seems dark under the cloudy sky. Still, there are a few blue patches to the west and south that just can't seem to work their way across the Strait of Georgia.

The lower lake is relatively flat, and there is brightening to the north, near Cassiar Island. We pass John's Cabin Number 4 in smooth water. Then, another kilometre to the north, it begins to get choppy. The wind shifts noticeably to the northwest, which is both good news and bad. The good news is that this clearly marks the passage of the frontal system. The bad news is that the choppiness is because the winds from the northwest are stronger than I expected.

We come abeam John's Cabin Number 1 in increasingly uncomfortable conditions. Waves whack at the hull. Fortunately, the distance between swells is short, which makes the depths of the troughs less extreme. The wind, which is now more from the north than the northwest, is an increasing problem. We call such winds a CB CB'er, a Chippewa Bay Cabin Buster. It wreaks havoc on cabins which lie directly in its path, like Cabin Number 1.

In the fading light at the end of this stormy day, I watch waves cresting over John's breakwater. This cabin is our escape valve if we decide not to continue, but docking here doesn't look appealing. So we continue.

Farther north, the conditions get worse. If we can just get past the point that juts out beyond the Washout, things should begin to improve. Getting out of the blast emerging from Chippewa Bay is important, but to do so means navigating the narrow passage between Cassiar Island and the shore. That's not a pleasant option in these winds and the increasing darkness.

The trip to the cabin normally takes 20 minutes. With our progress hampered by the high waves, we've already consumed 30 minutes, and we're barely past the mid-point. At this rate, we'll be arriving at Hole in the Wall in total darkness.

Turning back is more than a psychological obstacle. I'd like to get to our cabin tonight, but there's more to it than that. For one thing, it's best to keep the bow pointed into the waves in large swells. Maneuvering broadside in order to turn around is not without risk. So to avoid the narrow channel near Cassiar and to keep the waves off the bow, I ease the boat to the left, away from the shore.

We're now in the midst of the blast from Chippewa Bay. The flashing white navigation light on Cassiar is well to our right, out of the primary blow, but I don't want to venture any closer. If we can just get past this island and then slip a bit to the east, we should be in more protected waters.

The Campion crashes into high waves that batter the hull with increasingly force. A few of these waves are at least 5 feet high, and that is well beyond my threshold of comfort. Groceries and supplies packed into the boat at the Shinglemill are being tossed around on the

floor behind us. Margy takes a moment to reach behind her to corral the contents of errant bags that have been emptied by the force of the pounding waves. I glance back, catching a glimpse of groceries that are sliding from one side of the stern to the other. A box of cereal is literally flying.

In this small boat, I've never experienced waves this big. In the increasing darkness, I can't see the water's surface more than a few feet in front of the boat. Maybe that's for the best. Waves splash over the bow, onto the windshield, and even through the closed canvas top that covers the boat. A gush of water pours into the canvas-covered bow and continues rearward past our feet. We're propelled upward only to come down with a resounding whack, and then it immediately begins all over again. Water splashes onto the windshield in sheets, and the wipers work hard to control the flow.

If I didn't have faith in this fiberglass hull, I'd swear this pounding would be enough to crack it open. The boat crashes down with such force that I feel my spine pushed upward with bone-jarring force. It's obvious we are near the limit of both our equipment and our boating skills.

The punishment is so severe that something in this boat could break. I hope it is not the engine. As difficult as it is to control the boat, an engine failure now would be disastrous. Immediately, we'd be twisted around broadside to the waves. Where or how we'd be pushed is not a thought I wish to dwell on. The good news is that this engine has been flawless in performance, with never even a sputter in hundreds of hours of operation. I pray it doesn't burp tonight.

"My wiper is gone!" shouts Margy.

When I glance over to her side of the boat, the windshield wiper is still attached, but not moving. It has been blown away from the glass and is wedged against the windshield frame. Margy is now even more blind than me. She's scared, and I know it. What she doesn't know is that I too am terrified. But at this moment, the safest route is straight ahead.

"Wiper's working again!" she yells.

"Good," I reply.

What the wind blows away, the waves wash back. It's nice to acknowledge even a minor improvement in our situation.

"It's a good boat," she adds.

You need to believe in something.

Just as it seems it can't get any worse without losing control of the boat, the waves begin to dissipate. Not only do they decrease in size, they almost disappear. It happens that fast.

We've passed the lip of Chippewa Bay and are now passing through the North Sea. Waves are usually worse here. But not tonight. A few minutes later, the green navigation light of First Narrows pops into view. We're almost home.

Beyond the Narrows, a large boom of logs is tied up to a cliff on the Goat Island side of the channel, abandoned by its tug. The captain has probably hot-footed it to town, seeking safety from the storm.

Navigating into the Hole at night, even in calm conditions, is not an enjoyable experience. But my trusty plug-in spotlight makes it more tolerable. I unzip the overhead canvas and stand with the light held high in one hand and my other hand on the boat's wheel down below. We slide safely through Cabin Number 3's breakwater entrance, and pull into our familiar parking spot.

Docked and ready to shutdown the engine, I turn the spotlight to the rear of the boat. Groceries are scattered everywhere. My light catches a plastic bottle of milk, a loaf of bread, two loose bananas, a box of cereal, and a jar of peanuts. A blueberry pie sits in the middle of the floor, upright and safe under its clear plastic lid.

Once aboard the float, I check for damage from the storm. One shore cable is severed, with all but one of its strands broken. Everything else is in good order. I check the rain gauge. It has rained 2.6 inches since we left yesterday. That's 66 millimetres, a lot of rain for a single storm, but not unheard of. What is more remarkable is the lake's water level, which I monitor using marks I've painted on the cliff. The water has risen nearly a full metre in the past 24 hours.

The water level of Powell Lake is more affected by runoff from the surrounding mountains than from falling rain. In the past week, with approximately 150 millimetres (6 inches) of rain, the lake has risen over two metres!

On the deck, five small cedar trees that I transplanted to coffee cans are lying on their sides. One of the trees has been ripped out of its container, never to be seen again.

I hoist the groceries out of the boat. Some items are still in their bags, but I unload most of the food item by item. Everything is soaked but nothing is ruined. It's a good thing we skipped the eggs.

Inside the cabin, I check the barometer. The pressure is 988 millibars and rising rapidly. The trend indicator bars show a long dip in barometric pressure over the past 12 hours, and then a sudden rise from 976 millibars within the past two hours. The V-shape pressure gradient confirms what has happened tonight. Looking back on it, leaving the Shinglemill this evening was a poor decision. But you make your choices, and you take your chances. And from that, you learn. Tonight we are home safely, and never have I appreciated this cabin more.

* * * * *

The next morning, under calm conditions, I cruise in the Campion to a nearby waterfall on Goat Island to watch the water tumble down the ravine. Then I motor into First Narrows and look south in the bright sunshine towards a tranquil North Sea.

Later in the afternoon, I hop aboard the Campion again for another brief trip to evaluate the flow down the nearby falls. I turn on the blower, but it sounds faint and puny. Then I hit the starter switch. There is a faint click, followed by nothing. The electrical system is completely dead. I check the obvious, crawling under the instrument panel to inspect the master fuse and circuit breakers. A glance in the aft compartment reveals a battery with a broken cable post. The battery cable must have been hanging on so precariously that my short trip over to the waterfalls earlier today was the last straw. Apparently, just as I bounced up against the cabin dock upon my return, the cable fell completely free. There's little doubt where and when the damage occurred. It would have required a violent blow. This chapter could have turned out different. Or maybe not written at all. It's enough to make you ponder the meaning of "luck."

* * * * *

It's not only wind that causes havoc on the lake during winter. The lake's shoreline is a source of flotsam that becomes worse as the water level rises and pulls driftwood from the shore. This navigational hazard reaches its peak during winter, when the snow melt and rain pour off the mountains, raising the level of the lake.

Low visibility on Powell Lake is another hazard. Low lying fog isn't common, but it's a condition that demands respect (*Up the Lake*, Chapter 9). Another source of low visibility is the occasional winter snowstorm that can produce whiteout conditions.

"Maybe we should get out of here," I say to Margy as soon as we hear the 6 am weather report on the local radio station.

Comox has already closed its schools for the day, although the overnight snowfall at Hole in the Wall has been only moderate. The report from Port Hardy is grim, with heavy snow already accumulating, and the storm is moving rapidly down Vancouver Island. The forecast for Powell River calls for snow to become heavy by mid-morning and to continue throughout the day. If we don't leave the cabin soon, we may face deteriorating road conditions in town. Additionally, wind is expected to become a problem by mid-day. This storm, as is typical in winter, will back into Powell River on strong southeast winds.

"Okay, let's pack up and get going," says Margy.

I know this is as hard for her as it is for me. We hate to leave our floating home under any conditions. Today, we had planned to stay at

the cabin until late afternoon, snatching some extra hours on the lake before we have to return to the States tomorrow. The weather forecast went downhill overnight, indicating that the approaching storm may be stronger than expected. There's no question that we should leave as soon as possible. Still, it is difficult.

We pack up under the light of a propane lantern. While Margy defrosts the refrigerator with boiling water, I heat more water on the stove for deicing of the Campion's windshield. The thermometer reads minus 7 Celsius. Snow has fallen off and on for three days, and the deck is now covered with almost a foot.

The Campion is frozen solid and covered over the top with a layer of powder. I use a broom to brush most of the snow off the canvas, and an ice scraper to clear the windows.

Unsnapping the boat's canvas cover requires hot water on the fasteners, and the dock ropes' are frozen into unmanageable knots. A little warm water does wonders.

I withhold the last bucket of heated water for the windshield. The air is so cold that I avoid dumping the water on too early, for fear it will refreeze before we get underway.

I start the boat 15 minutes before we depart, giving the engine plenty of time to warm up. This also provides time for the defroster (a modified hair-dryer) and the windshield cold-air blower (a bilge blower modified by John) to clear the windshield.

I walk around the cabin one last time, checking that all is secure. Then I apply the warm water to it. The glass clears perfectly, but it won't last. Finally we're aboard and on our way.

"Did you turn off the propane?"

"Damn!"

We're only a few metres from the dock, but already we must go back.

I try backing against the dock, but I am too far out of position. So I pull around in a tight circle and finally get back into position. I hop onto the deck, turn off the propane, and we try again. This time we get the same short distance from the dock when I remember something else we've forgotten.

"Poor Buoy Boy," I say, when I notice the toy racing buoy, still tied to the breakwater, steadfastly protecting us from intruders.

"He'll get awfully cold, waiting a month for us to return in the middle of winter," replies Margy.

We wouldn't think of leaving our reliable buoy on his own for that long. While I attempt to untie Buoy Boy from his tether at the breakwater entrance, the boat bumps clumsily against the log boom. I leave my gloves on to protect my hand from the cold as I reach into the water to grab the anchor ring. I wrap up the rope, and jam Buoy Boy under the passenger seat. Then, I swap my soaked gloves for a dry pair. Finally, we are ready to go.

By now, the wind is picking up and the snowfall has increased in intensity, both earlier than forecast. The previously warm water on the windshield has already frozen to a frosty coat, so I unzip the overhead canvas and stick my head out to scrape spots clear on my windshield and also on Margy's side.

We exit the Hole and manage to get up on-plane while there is still adequate forward visibility. As we pass through First Narrows, the falling snow turns into a horizontal curtain of white. The good news is that the wind has not yet whipped the lake's surface into big waves, and it is a short distance to the Shinglemill.

The windshield wipers face a losing battle. My hair-dryer defroster gives me a tiny clear spot, but I have to hunch awkwardly forward to peer through it.

"We'll need to dead reckon across the North Sea," I say, trying to sound confident.

We know our way around this part of the lake, but flying blind is never comfortable in a boat.

"I'll watch for logs," says Margy.

Her windshield, without a defroster, is in worse shape than mine, but she has good eyes.

"There won't be much traffic today," I remind her. "But keep a close lookout for work boats. Tugs too."

It isn't a pleasant prospect. Even a good mental map of the lake's shoreline won't help in a head-to-head encounter with a boat or log. There will be little advance notice if we come upon either in the near-zero visibility.

Because of the iced up windows, there's no visibility to the sides and rear. I figure we are aimed just to the right of Cassiar Island, but

I see no sign of land ahead. The waves are picking up, but we're still well within our limits.

After five minutes of this, I expect to see land – Cassiar or the east shoreline. But neither has appeared.

"I'm going to do a three-sixty to try to pick up a landmark," I say.

"Okay, we should be able to find something," replies Margy.

Two intelligent people, knowledgeable regarding the local shoreline, and with reasonable experience in boats, have just made a major error that could be costly.

I catch the blunder as soon as I'm established in the turn. There are no landmarks to see in any direction, and that means I need to be sure I roll out on the same heading I was on when I started. But all we have is a compass that we can't trust in rough conditions. (Embarrassingly, it's a compass not to be trusted in smooth conditions either.) I roll out of the turn when I "guess" we have completed a 360-degree turn. (Margy later reports she felt we made at least two complete circles.)

Landfall is far overdue, but we press on. I deviate 30 degrees to the left to assure we hit land on the east side of the lake, which should be the protected side in these southeast winds. Regardless of our circling maneuver, I'm convinced we are headed towards the east shore.

"There's the palm tree!" yells Margy, sounding very relieved.

Of course, there are no palm trees on this lake, but I know exactly what she means. In front of us is a steeply-leaning fir on a point of land. It's a promontory we know well, where our solitary "palm tree" sticks out into the lake. We pass close to it on nearly every trip up and down Powell Lake. To see our palm tree now sends a thrill up my spine.

But the tree doesn't look quite right. I want to believe this is our palm tree, it's shape distorted by today's unusually low visibility.

"Maybe it isn't the palm tree," says Margy, as we slide past the point.

"But there's no other place with a tree like that on the east shore of the lake," I counter.

I still want to believe. The shore is to our left, so this must be the east shore. What could be going on here?

"Oh, oh," spurts Margy.

As she speaks, I simultaneously recognize what she sees in front of us. First Narrows is nearly straight ahead. The promontory with the

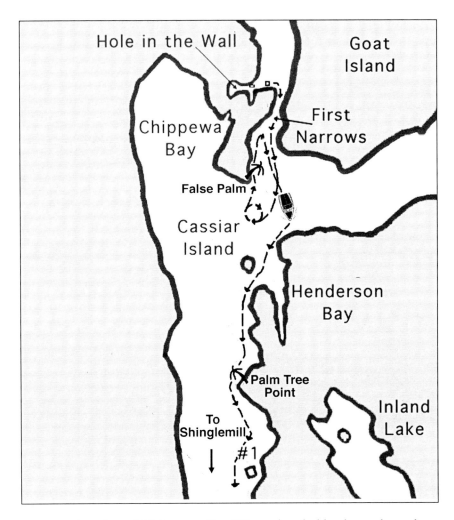

tree was the edge of Chippewa Bay. We are headed back north, and are almost back to our cabin. Our route south and then back north again must look like the path of a drunken sailor.

We consider continuing through the Narrows, returning to the cabin, and postponing our departure until after the storm passes. Still, we want to get back to town before the real storm begins, and we can. So I turn the Campion around, out again into the North Sea, sticking to my heading this time. We make it across to Cassiar Island without making any more errant circles, pass the palm tree on the point, and are docked at the Shinglemill before the southeast blast reaches full force. The road to town is still passable, and all ends well.

But you'll never find me on the lake again in low visibility without a good compass or GPS. And my circling days are, hopefully, behind me. Every trip up and down the lake, the palm tree serves as a gentle reminder.

Chapter 15

Docks, Logs, and Labour Day

"Want to go up towards Olsen's and pick up a dock?" asks John, soon after arriving at Cabin Number 3 in his Hourston.

I know the dock he's talking about. The damaged structure is moored just beyond the Clover Lake logging area. The winter storms have taken their toll on many cabins, and this dock is one of the casualties. Since it was the only dock for the adjacent cabin, its loss has cost the owner dearly. As I understand it, the dock is completely unusable. John plans to bring it down to Cabin Number 1 in the south section of the lake for repairs.

"Sure. Let's take the Campion. It'll tow the dock easier," I reply.

The Campion's counter-rotating twin props, mounted on a stern drive, create a powerful thrust, better than John's outboard motor. It will be a slow trip in any boat, but the Campion will be able to tow the dock down the lake a bit faster.

"I've got extra gas," says John. "I'll bring it just in case."

We load up the Campion – tools, lunch sacks, pike poles, rope, extra gas, two men, and one dog. Off we go.

The trip up the lake is fast, with calm winds that are so typical this time of year. It's always best to get started early, because these conditions won't last long. Summer daytime inflow winds usually begin to whip up the water by early afternoon.

We tie up against the damaged dock. It's in even worse shape than I expected. John hasn't been able to determine the cost of repairs, so the cabin owner hasn't yet approved the renovation. I'm certain any repairs made by John will be both top quality and relatively inexpensive. But, at first glance, I can hardly imagine where John will begin.

"It's a pile of crap," I say. "How will you ever rebuild this?"

"Not much left to rebuild. I'll have to throw a lot of it away and use new lumber. Won't know what I've got until I start pulling it apart."

"I can tell you what you've got," I reply. "A mess."

We set about trying to disconnect what's left of the dock from the shore. The structure is (was) the dock leading to a cabin built on land, providing breakwater-like protection as well as a place to park several boats. Now it's a pile of wind-damaged wood, tied loosely to the rocks. But not loose enough to disconnect easily.

After we unhook several chains and ropes that hold the floating structure in place, one troublesome chain remains. We work at it for a while before John finally gives up and turns to his gas-driven grinder. It's a modified chainsaw that spins a huge grinding blade. Sparks fly, as John severs the final link to shore.

"That should do it," says John. "We'll hook up the Campion and see if we can pull it away."

All of the obvious connections are gone, but the dock still rebounds back towards the cabin when John shoves it away with his pike pole. The dock may be dragging some old cables.

It isn't often that I get the chance to pull a structure as large as this dock, although I've helped John on such projects many times. John is the captain on these occasions – I'm only along for the ride. But today he wants to stay on the dock while I try to break it loose with the boat. From that position, John will be able to detect problem spots, and use his pike pole to assist with any jams.

I take my job seriously, hooking up the tow rope and positioning the Campion in a straight line away from the dock. When I'm finally where I think I should be, I take up the slack in the line and wave to John.

"Hit it!" he yells.

I push the throttle forward about half-way, waiting for some sign of movement. The boat creeps slowly forward as the rope stretches, but the dock doesn't budge. Something is still holding us to shore. Over my shoulder I see John rushing around on the dock, pushing at suspected spots with his pike pole. When I add a little more power, there is a surge of forward movement, and we are free. I look back at the dock, as it moves out and away from the cabin. John is poised on the rubble heap with his pike pole held high, looking like Moses at the parting of the Red Sea.

I throttle back to idle, then neutral, and climb back onto the swim grid. Arm over arm, I pull on the rope, bringing the floating dock closer to the boat. Once it is floating freely, even a big raft can be easily handled. Within a few minutes, John is back in the boat and in the captain's seat. Off we go, slow but sure, down the lake.

We travel at less than five knots, and the inflow headwind is already creating waves. I toss out my fishing line, using a small red-and-white daredevil to troll near the surface. Sure enough, coming around Elvis Rock, I hook a small trout.

It takes nearly three hours to make it back to Hole in the Wall, where we temporarily tie the towed dock to the breakwater at John's Cabin Number 2. By now, the wind has risen further, with whitecaps beginning to build, hindering any further progress down the lake to Cabin Number 1. We'll finish the tow tomorrow.

* * * * *

John arrives at Hole in the Wall early the next morning, ready to finish the tow. We'll use the Campion again, tying John's Hourston to the ugly wooden pile that was once called a dock. We pull both in tandem. When we finally make it to Cabin Number 1, I can return to Hole in the Wall in the Campion, while John uses his Hourston to return to town.

As we slip through First Narrows towards Cassiar Island, the winds are light. I play out the line in my fishing reel, again trolling for trout.

This is the perfect pace for life on the lake. Do a little work, play a little, spend some time with a friend, and travel slowly.

* * * * *

Margy and I cruise up the lake past John's Cabin Number 4, also known as the "Toolbox," located only two kilometres from the Shinglemill. As always, we travel close enough to John's cabins to inspect them as we pass by on each trip. You never know what you'll find.

The door to the Toolbox stands open. I ease in closer, but see no boat inside the breakwater.

I finally spot John's tin boat wedged in between his stash of floating logs. On closer inspection, I see John kneeling on his dock, where a huge log is tethered by a thick yellow rope.

I've been inside this breakwater a few times, though my visits to the Toolbox have been rare. The small floating red shed is little more than a place-keeper, to hold the site for a future floating cabin. As I angle into the breakwater's narrow entrance, Margy yells out: "Stump!"

She points in the direction of a submerged trunk that I don't see. I angle the boat away from the spot and cut the throttle, shifting into neutral. We drift past the obstacle, and Margy points ahead again: "Another one!" she yells.

We zigzag to the front of the Toolbox, past the dock where the big log and tin boat are tied. John meets us at the corner of the Box, reaching out to grab our bow line.

"Watch out for those stumps," says John. "They'll get you."

I've never been aboard this small float before, but I can see that it is more elaborate than I thought. Through the open door of the Toolbox, I notice that it really is a tool shed, with rows of shelves and assorted junk leaning up against the walls.

"Quite the place," I say.

"Watch out when you step aboard," says John. "Lots of bad boards. Walk where you see the nails."

As soon as I'm up on the deck, I see what he means. Many of the cedar deck boards are rotten and broken through. If you step on the beams, where you see the nails, it's plenty strong. Otherwise, your foot could go right through.

"What are you doing with the log?" asks Margy, as she steps carefully from beam to beam.

The large cedar log, over a foot in diameter and about 40 feet long, looks nearly big enough to be used in a float cabin foundation. John accumulates logs of all types and sizes, but big cedars are his favourite. All of his cabins are used as floating storage for logs waiting to discover their eventual purpose. If nothing else, these logs can be used to reinforce John's breakwaters, which are some of the sturdiest on the lake.

"I'm cutting a hole in the end to insert a chain," he replies. "Sounds easy, but it takes a good-sized hole to hold a big chain."

Margy and I (and Bro) watch John, as he sharpens the blades of his chainsaw, sliding the small metal file across each blade in sequence. When he's ready to go back to work, I hop down to the dock with him. Margy sits on the deck, her feet dangling over the side, giving Bro the attention he deserves.

I glance into the tin boat that floats nearby, and notice that it is filled with water, more than usual. John has cruised down here from Cabin Number 1, and this tin boat leaks so much that it fills quickly, unless you continually bail it out.

John fires up his saw and goes back to work, while I assist by holding the log tight against the dock. He makes another long horizontal cut at the end of the log to form a bench for the hole he will make. Using a saw at this angle for such a long slice is nearly impossible. If I were to try such a cut, the chainsaw would surely jamb after cutting only a few inches, but somehow John holds the saw perfectly level. The blades go

through the wood smoothly, without any binding. Then he makes a short vertical cut to release the slab and create the bench for the hole.

"Now the tough part," John says.

He lifts his chainsaw vertical to make the first cut for the hole that will go all the way through the log. The saw's bar looks barely long enough to make it through to the other side, and keeping a chainsaw perfectly vertical while cutting is a difficult maneuver.

Amazingly, the saw slides down through the log with ease (at least from the standpoint of the observer). The blades strike the water below the log just as the bar of the chainsaw reaches its extremity, spraying water up and out of the new hole.

"Just long enough," says John, with a smile.

When he's finished with the four cuts on the square hole, he uses his pike pole to tap down on the newly created core. The wooden plug pops down and out of the log.

"Let's turn the log around so I can notch the other end," says John.

"Doesn't look like enough room," I say.

"No problem," says John. "I think it will just fit."

He hops into his tin boat, sloshes through the water to the stern, and yanks on the motor's starter cord. The old engine starts on the

first pull. I untie the bow, while John bails a few scoops of water out of the stern with a cut-off bleach bottle. While I hold onto one end of the log, he maneuvers the leaky boat to the other end and gives it a gentle pull.

Without further adjustment, the log slowly swings around. As John turns the tin boat to follow, he yells to me: "Can you walk your end down to the end of the dock?"

I push on the log, and it moves along the dock. As it slips around the corner, the other end has nearly reached the breakwater. It clears by only a few inches.

"Close, but it'll work," says John.

When the log is back in position against the dock, John begins the same cutting process on the other end. Once again, his cuts are level and precise. Within a few minutes, he is dropping a heavy chain through the new hole, in preparation for securing the log to the breakwater. Then he is back aboard his tin boat, dragging the big log out towards its newly assigned spot on the log boom.

How John is able to accomplish such heavy tasks all by himself is amazing, but he does such work all the time. Sometimes I am able to assist by merely holding a log or handing him tools. Yet most of the time he completes heavy and difficult tasks unassisted. John's scope of knowledge regarding anything that floats is immense – the ultimate aquatic engineer.

* * * * *

Labour Day, sad day. It marks the unofficial end to summer, but here at Hole in the Wall, the end is more ominous. After today, much of the marine support system for boaters in coastal British Columbia will shut down. The tourists will be gone. In California, summer can extend well into October. Here, on the coast of British Columbia, summer is over even before the September equinox arrives.

This Labour Day is even sadder than normal, for I am going back to the States. This will be my last day on the float for more than a month, and such milestones are not taken lightly. When I close up the cabin, a melancholy mood can easily slip into near-depression.

Leaving my floating home is never easy, but even more so today. I've been alone on the float all weekend, and I've had the Hole almost to myself. Three nearby cabins were occupied yesterday, but this morning they were vacated when the ceaseless rain continued to fall.

As far as I can tell (most neighboring cabins are blocked from my view by granite cliffs), no one remains in the Hole except me. I love it that way. But I face the process of closing up the cabin with remorse.

I've packed up to leave the cabin so many times that the process is nearly automatic. The work of closing up doesn't bother me. Instead, what bothers me is the fear that I may never be able to come back to this place that I love so much. Such fears are flawed, as I remind myself each time I return. Yet, my qualms regarding departure persist.

This afternoon, I intend to extract every ounce of enjoyment from my final day. I've completed most of the get-ready-to-leave tasks, pulling the floating pool toys out of the water, moving equipment to the shed, and defrosting the refrigerator. About all that remains is to remove Mr. Buoy Boy from his guard position (tethered to the breakwater entrance), pull the tin boat up onto the dock, and turn off the propane and electricity. These sad tasks mark the end of my stay, so I delay doing them as long as possible.

Meanwhile, the rain continues to fall in a magnificent display of "miserable" weather. Margy and I love that word, since we know that is how much of the rest of the world reacts to persistent rain. We thrive on the beauty of the rain, while holed up in our comfortable cabin: "Just miserable, isn't it?" we kid each other.

According to the satellite radio, the temperature at my home in California reached 42 degrees C today, triple digits on the Fahrenheit scale. I don't miss it a bit.

I sit on the sofa, with a grand view of Goat Island and First Narrows. The fireplace keeps me warm on this 16-degree day at the end of summer. The radio is tuned to a classical station, the only kind of music I can listen to when I write. Some days my writing flows rapidly, and today is one of those days. Probably, it's my melancholy mood, coupled with the "miserable" weather.

I hear a voice – must be the radio. No one is within several kilometres of the cabin. No, it is a voice. And now there's a head – bobbing up and down off the front deck.

I put the laptop aside and stand up. The head turns into a full body, standing in a light green canoe. So someone is here after all.

"Hello!" yells Cameron, standing in front of me, shouting through the closed glass door. "Sorry to bother you."

I slide open the door and greet my neighbor.

"No problem," I say. "I thought I heard a voice. Figured I was going crazy."

Cameron laughs, and then runs his hand through his bushy blond hair, soaked from the lightly falling rain. He looks like he's in trouble.

"I need to ask a favour," he says.

"Of course. What can I do?" I reply.

This is one place where there is no doubt what you will do if someone needs help. People don't ask unless they need to. And if they need help, everyone is quick to respond.

"Do you have any jumper cables?" asks Cameron. "The battery in my boat is dead. Maybe we can use your boat to jump-start it."

"No regular jumper cables, but I've got a generator with a set of cables that will do the trick. Let me get dressed."

I'm dressed, but not for the rain. So I quickly pull on my rain suit, a jacket, and shoes. I grab my life vest and head out the door. Cameron has moved his canoe around to the dock at the side of the cabin, waiting for me.

"You go ahead," I say. "I'll grab the generator and cables and meet you at your cabin."

Cameron seems relieved that he doesn't need to wait for me any longer in the rain. He acknowledges with a "Thanks!" and immediately starts paddling away to the back of the Hole.

I grab the gas generator from the shed, along with the cables. Within a few minutes, I've loaded the bulky generator into the tin boat and am on my way. As I motor back into the Hole, I can see Cameron's boat docked at his cabin. On the deck, a little girl walks back and forth in a red life vest. Probably everyone was ready to leave when this happened.

It feels good to be rescuing fellow cabin dwellers, and even better to feel that I actually know what I'm doing. (It hasn't always been that way.)

As I pull up to the dock, Cameron grabs my bow line. I hand him the generator, and he sets it down near the stern of his boat. *Budweiser* is written in big blue letters on his bow. This is a powerful motor, but now it is dead in the water.

"I'll get the generator going," I say. "Here, you can hook up these cables. Black is negative, if you can find the proper terminal."

Cameron looks at me like I am from outer space. I guess he's aware of what black and red cables mean.

"The cables are puny," I say, as I pull on the generator's starter cord. "So we probably won't be able to start the boat directly from the generator. But it should take only a few minutes to get you recharged."

As Cameron connects the cables to the battery in the stern, I notice two bigger batteries sitting on the floor near the rear seat. Next to them is a large yellow booster pack with hefty jumper cables built in.

"Looks like you've got lots of spare power," I say, wondering if the boat's battery may not be the starting problem.

"Not any good though," he says. "I've tried these – they're all dead. I know it's my battery. I killed it running the stereo."

As soon as the generator is running and the cables are connected, he tries the ignition switch. Click-click, the solenoid is trying, but without enough power to rotate the starter.

"Can't give you enough power for a jump start through these tiny wires," I say. "But your battery should charge up. Just give it a few minutes."

Cameron nods, fiddles some more with the cable connections, and tries again. This time, the click-click is gone. The starter struggles but barely rotates.

"Almost there," I say.

This is going to work, and it will make both of us very happy.

After waiting another few minutes, the engine starts nicely. Cameron works at the throttle to keep the throaty motor running. Once it's operating smoothly, he disconnects the cables and walks to the front of the boat to check the instrument panel.

"The alternator is charging," he reports, meaning that the problem is solved and the engine will keep running.

Mission accomplished. I've saved the day. It's a mighty good feeling.

As I drive away from Cameron's cabin, I head for Mr. Buoy Boy, and then disconnect him from his guard-the-float position. After storing the toy racing buoy under the seat, I speed across to the nearby waterfalls on Goat Island, where I stop for a moment and look up through the narrow canyon. At this time of year, thick bushes cover the ravine. Just a slice of the falls is still visible, tumbling downward towards the lake.

From here, I continue south, pushing at full throttle in the light rain. The tin boat glides only a few metres from vertical cliffs, down into the opening of First Narrows. As I pass Hole in the Wall, *Budweiser* is powering its way out. Cameron's engine sounds healthy, and he waves through the opening in his boat's overhead canvas. I wave back, passing behind (*whack-whack* over the wake), towards the green navigation light on the bluff.

I swing sharply at the light, parallel the shore back towards the Hole, and return to my cabin. Entering the breakwater, I position the tin boat at the end of the dock, using the power of the small outboard to push it partway up onto the deck. I hop out and muscle the boat the rest of the way, remove the drain plug, and secure the tie-down lines. I remove the generator and cables, along with the cruise-a-day gas tank, carrying them to the shed for use in another season.

The tin boat is high and dry, ready for my next visit. I'm confident that I will be back.

◊ ◊ ◊ ◊ ◊ ◊

Epilogue

On the Lake

When you come from a city, especially one as fast-paced as Los Angeles, a float cabin on Powell Lake is quite a change. When that cabin evolves from being a recreational cottage to an established home, it turns the heads of locals who are much hardier than me. Most float cabins on Powell Lake are used as part-time getaways. For me, it's home.

The last census showed that Fritz, a local legend on the lake, was Powell Lake's only year-round resident. Now you can add me to that list. You'll find me on the lake in all seasons. If you live in Los Angeles where there is really only one season, you appreciate living on the lake even more.

I have a condo in Powell River, and that is where many of my friends expect to find me. But it is not where I want to live. I can easily do without running water, TV, and the Internet. Occasional doses of all three, during visits to town, are a nice luxury.

In recent years, the basics of life have become more important to me. A woodstove and a natural swimming pool take on new importance. My big-screen TV is the ever-changing view out of my patio door, looking east towards Goat Island and First Narrows. A tug towing a barge up the lake is always worth close inspection. A floatplane scud-running south to the Shinglemill provides a stop-what-you're-doing moment. A waterfall plummeting down the face of Goat Island never loses its impact.

One summer day, a two-person kayak glides into Hole in the Wall, passing close to my breakwater. Meanwhile, I sit inside my cabin, the screen door open to let in the warmth of the afternoon air. Voices of the paddlers carry effortlessly over the water.

"Cute little garden," says the woman in the front of the kayak.

"Yes, vegetables, it looks like," replies the man in the back.

Their conversation pauses as they paddle with synchronized strokes. They ease out of view, continuing farther back into the Hole. But their voices still carry clearly.

"A place like this must get real boring," adds the woman. "I'd just go crazy after a while."

Yes, this is not for everyone. But I am never bored. This lake has slipped into the depth of my being. It permeates all that I am. It is my home.

About the Author

From 1980 to 2005, Wayne Lutz was Chairman of the Aeronautics Department at Mount San Antonio College in Los Angeles. He led the college's Flying Team to championships as Top Community College in the United States seven times. He has also served 20 years as a U.S. Air Force C-130 aircraft maintenance officer. His educational background includes a B.S. degree in physics from the University of Buffalo and an M.S. in systems management from the University of Southern California.

The author is a flight instructor with 7000 hours of flying experience. For the past three decades, he has spent summers in Canada, exploring remote regions in his Piper Arrow, camping next to his airplane. The author resides in a floating cabin on Canada's Powell Lake and in a city-folk condo in Los Angeles. His writing genres include regional Canadian publications and science fiction. The author's next books, *Up the Inlet* and *Farther Up the Main,* are scheduled for publication in mid-2009.

Up the Lake
Up the Main
Up the Winter Trail
Up the Strait
Up the Airway
Farther Up the Lake

Order books in this series at:
www.PowellRiverBooks.com

Free Audio Chapters for the first 6 books
in this series are now available at the
Powell River Books web site

Reader's can email the author at:
wlutz@mtsac.edu

Coastal BC Living
Blog — PowellRiverBooks.blogspot.com

Farther Up the Lake is the sixth in a series of volumes focusing on the unique places and memorable people of coastal British Columbia